Paper F6

**Taxation
(Finance Act 2016)**

For June 2017 to March 2018 examination sittings

Pocket notes

British library cataloguing-in-publication data

A catalogue record for this book is available from the British Library.

Published by:
Kaplan Publishing UK
Unit 2 The Business Centre
Molly Millars Lane
Wokingham
Berkshire
RG41 2QZ

ISBN 978-1-78415-712-8

© Kaplan Financial Limited, 2016

Printed and bound in Great Britain.

The text in this material and any others made available by any Kaplan Group company does not amount to advice on a particular matter and should not be taken as such. No reliance should be placed on the content as the basis for any investment or other decision or in connection with any advice given to third parties. Please consult your appropriate professional adviser as necessary. Kaplan Publishing Limited and all other Kaplan group companies expressly disclaim all liability to any person in respect of any losses or other claims, whether direct, indirect, incidental, consequential or otherwise arising in relation to the use of such materials.

Contents

KAPLAN PUBLIS

Preface

These notes contain the key points you need to know for the exam, presented in a unique visual way that makes revision easy and effective.

Written by experienced lecturers and authors, these notes break down content into manageable chunks to maximise your concentration.

Throughout these notes you will find references to past questions including the name of the question in the Kaplan exam kit. These have been included to enable you to locate the questions in the exam kit. Please be aware that due to changes in the examination format in the past two years, all questions have been adapted from their orginal format in order to be representative of the format and style of questions that you are likely see in your F6 examination. Therefore, there may be differences between the Kaplan examination version and the version available on the ACCA website, which will not have been updated to current examination format.

Quality and accuracy are of the utmost importance to us so if you spot an error in any of our products, please send an email to mykaplanreporting@kaplan.com with full details, or follow the link to the feedback form in MyKaplan.

Our Quality Co-ordinator will work with our technical team to verify the error and take action to ensure it is corrected in future editions.

The examination

F6 is a three hour 15 minute assessment, available as a paper-based examination. The ACCA also introduced a computer-based examination from September 2016 in certain markets.

The computer–based examination is three hours and 20 minutes with effect from the March 2017 sitting. The increase of 20 minutes in comparison to earlier examinations is to incorporate 'seeded content'. These questions do not contribute to your overall mark but ensure that the examinations are fair and reliable.

The paper will consist of 3 compulsory sections A, B and C.

Section A will be comprised of 15 multiple-choice questions of 2 marks each.

Section B will be comprised of 3 objective test (OT) case questions with five OT questions worth 2 marks each linked to each case.

Section C will be comprised of one 10 mark and two 15 mark constructed response (long questions.

The two 15 mark questions will focus on income tax (syllabus area B) and the other corporation tax (syllabus area E).

The section A questions, section B question and the 10 mark section C question can cover any areas of the syllabus.

Differences between the paper-based and computer-based examination

In the paper-based examination, all of the OT questions in section A and B will be of multiple choice style, with one correct answer from a choice of four.

In the computer-based examination the OT questions in section A and B will be in a variety of different styles including multiple choice.

Section C will be the same format for both versions of the examination.

Aims and capabilities

Aim of the paper

To develop knowledge and skills relating to the tax system as applicable to individuals, single companies, and groups of companies.

Main capabilities

On successful completion of this paper candidates should be able to:

- explain the operation and scope of the tax system and the obligations of taxpayers and/or their agents and the implications of non-compliance

- explain and compute the income tax liabilities of individuals and the effect of national insurance contributions (NICs) on employees, employers and the self-employed

- explain and compute the chargeable gains arising on individuals

- explain and compute the inheritance tax liabilities of individuals

- explain and compute the corporation tax liabilities of individual companies and groups of companies

- explain and compute the effects of value added tax on incorporated and unincorporated businesses.

The keys to success in paper F6

Paper F6 is divided into three different sections, requiring the application of different skills to be successful.

If you decide to use 15 minutes for reading and planning, you should allocate 1.8 minutes per mark for the remaining 3 hours of the examination.

If you are sitting an F6 CBE, the time available for your examination will be different from the time available for the paper-based examination so your time allocation for each mark will also be different.

Section A

Applying the timing principle of 1.8 minutes per mark for F6 means that 15 objective test (OT) questions (30 marks) should take 54 minutes.

Work steadily. Rushing leads to careless mistakes and questions are designed to include answers which result from careless mistakes.

If you don't know the answer, eliminate those options you know are incorrect and see if the answer becomes more obvious.

Remember that only one answer to an OT question can be right and there is no negative marking for an incorrect answer.

After you have eliminated any options that you know to be wrong, if you are still unsure, guess.

Section B

Each case has five 2 mark OT questions linked to it, meaning that each case is worth 10 marks in total. You should therefore spend 18 minutes (10 x 1.8 minutes) tackling each case.

Read the information relating to each case carefully.

Firstly, identify any OT questions that can be answered without significant workings and attempt these. Use your remaining time to attempt the OT questions that require workings.

The above guidance for section A is equally valid for the section B OT questions.

Section C

Always show workings in questions.

Always state any assumptions you make if you do not understand what the question is asking.

Learn and follow the pro formas for computational questions.

Adopt a logical approach and cross reference workings to the main computation to keep your paper tidy.

All sections

Don't skip parts of the syllabus in your studies. The F6 paper has 33 different questions that contribute to your overall mark so the examination can cover a very broad selection of the syllabus each sitting.

Spend time learning the rules and definitions

Read the F6 examining team's articles released in Student Accountant in the months up to your examination date. These give clues as to the areas that may be covered.

Practice plenty of questions to improve your ability to apply the techniques and perform the calculations.

Don't panic if you realise that you've answered a question incorrectly. Getting on question wrong will not mean the difference between passing and failing.

In the exam...

- Make sure you take all the stationery you will need and a spare calculator.

- Use your allocated reading and planning time carefully reading the section B and C questions in full.

- Decide the order in which to attempt the sections and stick to your plan.

- Work out the length of time you have to complete each question.

- Attempt all of the questions.

- Missing out questions makes it harder for you to achieve success – you still have to gain 50 marks!

- At the end of your time allocation, move on to the next question; if you have spare time at the end you can go back to any unfinished questions.

- Try to spend the last five minutes reading through your answers and making any additions or corrections.

For paper-based exams...

- Enter your answer for the section A and B OTs on the specific answer sheet provided.

- Always start each section C question on a new page.

- Don't write in the margins of the answer paper.

- Ideally use black ink or biro. Never write in red or green ink or pencil. Your script will be scanned before being sent electronically to the marker; any other colour does not scan well.

- Do not use correction fluid (e.g Tipp-Ex) in the exam. It does not scan well and the word written on it cannot be read.

For computer-based exams...

- Be sure you understand how to use the software before you start the examination. If in doubt, ask the assessment centre staff to explain it to you.

- Questions are displayed on screen and answers are entered using a keyboard and a mouse.

1

Income tax: overview and property income

In this chapter

- Tax year.
- Taxable income.
- Exempt income.
- Pro forma – income tax computation.
- Reliefs.
- Personal allowance.
- Child benefit tax charge.
- Calculating income tax.
- Tax rates.
- Tax deducted at source.
- Property income.
- Joint income.
- Accrued income scheme.
- Tax status.

Tax year

- An individual's taxable income is assessed in respect of a tax year.
- Runs from 6th April to following 5th April.

Tax year 2016/17: 6 April 2016 to 5 April 2017.

Taxable income

Income assessable	Basis of assessment
Profits from a trade/profession/vocation	Tax adjusted trading profits of the accounts ending in the current tax year
Interest received from UK sources	
Income from employment	Income received in the tax year
Dividend income	
Property income	Income accruing in the tax year

Income taxed at different income tax rates
depending on type of income:

Non-savings	Savings	Dividends
↓	↓	↓
Employment income	Interest income	Dividend income
Trading profits		
Property income		

Income must be included in computation
gross.

Note: Some interest is received net of tax, as
tax is withheld at source by the payer.
However, interest will always be received
gross in the F6 examination.

Exempt income

Main examples:

- Premium bond prizes.
- Betting/gambling winnings.
- Returns on NS&I certificates.
- Income received from ISAs.
- Repayment interest (interest on tax repayments).

Key Point

Any exempt income should be:

- excluded in the income tax computation
- but noted as exempt in section C exam answers.

Exam focus

Use the following income tax pro forma to ensure that income tax is calculated at the correct rates on different sources of income

Pro forma – Income tax computation – 2016/17

	Total £	Non-savings £	Savings £	Dividends £
Employment income	X	X		
Trading profits	X	X		
Property income	X	X		
Pension income	X	X		
Interest income	X		X	
Dividend income	X			X
Total income	X	X	X	X
Less: Reliefs	(X)	(X)		
Net income	X	X	X	X
Less: Personal Allowance (PA)	(11,000)	(11,000)		
Taxable income	X	X	X	X

Income tax computation

	£
Non-savings income x 20/40/45%	x
Savings income x 0/20/40/45% (Note)	x
Dividend income x 0/7.5/32.5/38.1% (Note)	x
Income tax liability	x
Less: PAYE	(x)
Income tax payable	**x**

The appropriate rate of tax depends on the level of taxable income:

Basic rate band limit = £32,000
Higher rate band limit = £150,000

Note: Savings income falling into the first £5,000 of taxable income is taxed at 0% (not 20%).

A savings nil rate band of £1,000 and £500 is available to basic and higher rate tax payers respectively.

A dividend nil rate band of £5,000 is available to all taxpayers.

Exam focus

Exam kit questions in this area:

OT case (section B) questions:

- Philip and Charles

Constructed response (section C) questions

- Patience
- Richard Tryer
- Samson and Delilah
- Chi Needle
- John Beach

Reliefs

- Reliefs are an allowable deduction from the total income of an individual, subject to a maximum amount.

- Main examples:

  - Qualifying interest

    Employees:
    interest on loans to purchase plant and machinery for use in employment

    Partners:
    interest on loans to purchase a share in a partnership or to contribute capital/loan to a partnership

  - Trading losses (Chapter 7).

- **Maximum amount of relief** deductible from total income is the **greater of**:

  - £50,000, or

  - 25% of adjusted total income.

Note that the maximum restriction will only be examined in the context of loss relief (see Chapter 7).

Personal allowance (PA)

- Available to all individuals.
- £11,000 for 2016/17.
- Deducted from net income to give taxable income.
- Lost if not used in the year.

Reduction of PA – higher rate taxpayers

- If adjusted net income (ANI) > £100,000:
  - reduce PA by:
    50% x (ANI – £100,000)
- If ANI > £122,000:
  - no PA
- Effective rate of tax on income between £100,000 to £122,000: 60%

- ANI is calculated as:

	£
Net income (per IT comp)	X
Less: Gross gift aid	(X)
Less: Gross personal pension contributions	(X)
ANI	X

Exam focus

Exam kit questions in this area:

OT case (section B) questions:

- Philip and Charles

Constructed response (section C) questions

- Samson and Delilah
- John Beach

Marriage Allowance (Transferable amount)

- A spouse or civil partner can elect to transfer a fixed amount of the PA to their spouse/civil partner.

- This is known as the marriage allowance (MA).

- Neither spouse/civil partner may be a higher or additional rate taxpayer.

Electing for the MA will be beneficial provided the transferor spouse/civil partner does not fully utilise their PA but the recipient spouse/civil partner does, so that their total income tax liability as a couple is reduced.

Method:

- The fixed amount of PA to transfer:
  - 10% of the individual's PA
  = £1,100 for 2016/17.

- There is no provision for transferring less than this amount.

- Relief is given by reducing the recipient's income tax liability by a maximum of £220 (i.e. £1,100 x 20% BR income tax).

Child benefit tax charge

A child benefit charge arises where:

- an individual receives child benefit, and
- they, or their spouse/civil partner, have adjusted net income (ANI) ≥ £50,000.

ANI = as for the restriction of the PA.

Income	Tax charge
£50,000 – £60,000	1% of child benefit for each £100 of income over £50,000
Over £60,000	The amount of child benefit received

Both the appropriate percentage and the tax charge are rounded down to the nearest whole number.

Where the charge applies the taxpayer must

- complete a tax return
- pay the charge through the self-assessment system.

The tax charge can be avoided by choosing not to claim child benefit.

Note that the child benefit (received from the government) should not be confused with childcare vouchers (received from an employer).

Calculating income tax

(1) Dividends, savings income and non-savings income need to be totalled separately.

(2) To ensure that tax is saved at the highest rates, reliefs and the PA should be deducted from:

- non-savings income
- then savings income
- then dividends.

(3) Order of calculation

Tax should be calculated in the same order:

- non-savings income
- then savings income
- then dividends.

Tax rates

- Different tax rates apply depending on the amount and type of income.

	Non-savings	Savings	Dividends
Basic rate band (first £32,000)	20%	20% (Note)	7.5% (Note)
Higher rate band (£32,001 – £150,000)	40%	40%	32.5%
Additional rate band (over £150,000)	45%	45%	38.1%

Note: If savings income falls into the first £5,000 of taxable income, it is taxed at 0% (not 20%).

A savings nil rate band is available as follows
- Basic rate taxpayers £1,000
- Higher rate taxpayers £500

All taxpayers are entitled to a £5,000 dividend nil rate band.

Pension contributions

- Personal pensions

  Relief for contributions paid by an individual into a personal pension scheme, is given as follows:

  - Paid net of basic rate tax (20%)
  - Basic and higher rate bands extended by the gross amount: (Amount paid x 100/80).

- Occupational pensions

  - Contributions deducted from employee's gross pay before PAYE is applied.

Charitable giving

Tax relief is available as follows:

- Gift aid scheme:
  - Paid net of basic rate tax (20%).
  - Basic and higher rate bands extended by the gross amount: (amount paid) x 100/80.
- Payroll deduction scheme
  - Donations deducted from employee gross pay before PAYE is applied.

Effect of extending bands

Income equivalent to gross personal pension contributions (PPC) and/or gross gift aid donations is

- taxed at 20% rather than 40% (if higher rate taxpayer) and in addition
- taxed at 40% rather than 45% (if an additional rate taxpayer).

This increases the amount of income taxed at a lower rate as opposed to a higher rate of tax.

Reduction of PA

In addition, remember that:

Gross PPCs and gift aid = also deducted from net income to arrive at ANI when comparing with the income limit for the reduction of the PA.

Exam focus

Exam kit questions in this area:

Constructed response (section C) questions

- Patience
- Richard Tryer
- Alfred King
- John Beach

Tax deducted at source

- If tax deducted at source exceeds the income tax liability, the excess is repayable.

Property income

- Taxes income from land and property.
- Calculated on an accruals basis for the tax year.
- Calculation of profits:

	£
Rental income	X
Less: Related expenses	(X)
Assessable income	X

- Expenditure is deductible if it is incurred 'wholly and exclusively' for the purposes of the letting (e.g. repairs, insurance, impairment loss).
- Interest paid = allowable deduction for individuals.
- Where there is more than one property the profits and losses from each property are aggregated.

- Taxed as non-savings income at:
  - 20%, 40% or 45%
- Property losses
  - for individuals, can only be carried forward against future property income.
- If a property is let furnished, the cost of replacement domestic items (i.e. not the original acquisition) is an allowable deduction.

Exam kit questions in this area:

Constructed response (section C) questions:

- Patience
- Leticia Stone
- Richard Tryer

Premiums for granting a short lease

Where a premium is paid on the grant of a short lease (≤ 50 years):

- Landlord is assessed on property income of:

	£
Premium	X
Less: 2% x premium x (n – 1)	(X)
Assessment on landlord	Y

where
n = number of years of lease.

Alternative calculation:

$$= \text{Premium} \times \left(\frac{51 - n}{50} \right)$$

Furnished holiday lettings (FHL)

- Assessed as property income but:
  - treated as arising from a single and separate trade.
- Advantages:
  - Business asset for CGT rollover relief, gift relief and entrepreneurs' relief.
  - Relevant earnings for pensions relief.
  - Capital allowances on all P&M including furniture.
- Any losses made on a qualifying FHL property may only be set against profits from other qualifying FHL properties.
  - firstly in the same tax year
  - then carried forward against future profits from FHL properties only.

- Conditions:
  - Let furnished on commercial basis.
  - Available to let for ≥ 210 days in the year.
  - Actually let for ≥ 105 days in the year.
  - Not let for periods of long-term occupation (occupied by same person > 31 days) in excess of 155 days in a year.

Rent-a-room relief

- Furnished room in a main domestic residence.
- Gross rents ≤ £7,500
  - exempt, unless elect for loss.
- Gross rents > £7,500
  - normal property income calculation unless elect for excess over £7,500 to be taxed (with no deduction for expenses).

Exam focus

Exam kit questions in this area:

Constructed response (section C) questions:

- Leticia Stone

Exam focus

Exam kit questions in this area:

Constructed response (section C) questions:

- Leticia Stone

Joint income

- Applies to married couples and civil partnerships.
- Normal assumption = 50/50 split.

Can elect for income to be taxed according to actual percentage ownership.

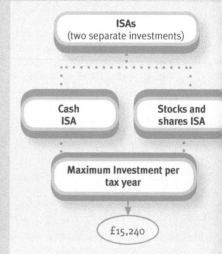

Accrued income scheme

Applies to individuals holding gilts with a total nominal value in excess of £5,000.

- Gains made on gilts by individuals are exempt.
- Without the scheme, interest accrued up to the date of sale would increase the value of the gilt and be included as part of the exempt gain.
- When the accrued income scheme applies, the **interest accrued up to the date of sale** will be treated as **savings income** for the individual selling the gilt.

Tax status

- All individuals resident in the UK = assessed to income tax on their **worldwide income** (UK and overseas).

Key Point

Knowledge of the residency definition is important. However in computational questions, the individual will always be:

- resident in the UK, and
- taxed on worldwide income.

Residence

Definition

An individual is resident in the UK for a tax year if they:

- do not meet one of the **automatic non-UK residence tests**, and
- meet one of the **automatic UK residence tests**, or
- meet one or more of the **sufficient ties tests**.

Resident in UK?

Automatic **non-UK residency tests**	Automatic **UK residency tests**	**Sufficient ties tests**

Individual in UK in **tax year** less than
• **16 days**, or
• **46 days** and not UK R for last 3 years, or
• **91 days** and works FT abroad
	Individual automatically UK R if:
	• In UK **183 days** in tax year, or
	• Only home in UK, or
	• Work FT in UK
		1 Close family
		  – Spouse/Civil partner/minor child
		2 Accommodation in UK
		  – used in tax year
		3 Substantive work in UK
		4 Days in UK in last two tax years
		  – › 90 days in either year
		5 Country tie – Most time spent in UK

Previously resident in UK
= UK R in one of last 3 years

Consider **all five** ties

See tax tables in exam

Not previously resident in UK
= not UK R in any of last 3 years

Consider **first four** ties

Application of sufficient ties test

Days spent in the UK	Previously resident (Leaver)	Not previously resident (Arriver)
Less than 16 days	Automatically **not** UK resident	Automatically **not** UK resident
16 to 45 days	Resident if: 4 UK ties (or more)	Automatically **not** UK resident
46 to 90 days	Resident if: 3 UK ties (or more)	Resident if: 4 UK ties
91 to 120 days	Resident if: 2 UK ties (or more)	Resident if: 3 UK ties (or more)
121 to 182 days	Resident if: 1 UK tie (or more)	Resident if: 2 UK ties (or more)
183 or more days	Automatically resident	Automatically resident

The above table is included in the tax rates and allowances provided to you in the examination. No other information relating to residence is included in the tax rates and allowances.

Sections A and B will almost certainly include some questions on income tax. In addition, one of the questions in section C will focus on income tax for 15 marks, and the 10 mark section C question may also include income tax aspects.

It is highly likely, therefore, that a question will involve the calculation of income tax liability or payable.

It is important that you familiarise yourself with the various types of income, along with the order in which they are taxed, and also how to apply the different rates of tax for interest and dividends.

As with all areas of the F6 syllabus, question practice is the key to success and is invaluable when it comes to taxing the different sources of income at the correct tax rates accurately under time pressure.

2

Employment income

In this chapter

- Employment v self-employment.
- Employment income.
- Benefits.
- Living accommodation.
- Company cars.
- Fuel benefit.
- Company vans.
- Beneficial loans.
- Use and transfer of assets.

Employment v self-employment

An employee works under a **contract of service** and a self-employed person under a **contract for services**.

The main criteria to look at when deciding between the two are:

- integration
- control
- financial risk
- equipment – who provides
- work performance and correction
- holidays and sickness benefits
- exclusivity.

Employment income

Basis of assessment

- Earnings are taxed on the receipts basis
  - Usually amounts are assessable for the tax year in which they are paid regardless of when earned.
  - An earlier 'received' date can apply for directors:
    - date when earnings are credited in the accounts, or
    - the end of the accounting period, where earnings are determined before the end of that period
    - date when earnings are determined, if after the end of the accounting period.

Employment income pro forma

	£
Salary/wages	x
Bonus	x
Benefits	x
	x
Less: Allowable deductions	(x)
Employment income	x

Allowable deductions

- Expenses specifically allowable:
  - contributions to registered occupational pension schemes
  - subscriptions to professional bodies
  - charitable donations under a payroll deduction scheme.
- Travel expenses are deductible if they are incurred necessarily in the performance of the duties of employment.
- Other expenses are deductible if they are incurred **wholly, exclusively and necessarily in the performance** of those duties.

Approved Mileage Allowance Payments (AMAP)

- Apply where an employee is paid a mileage allowance by the employer for using his own car for business travel.

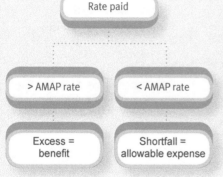

The AMAP rates are included in the tax rates and allowances provided to you in the examination.

Exam kit questions in this area:

Constructed response (section C) questions

- Leticia Stone
- John Beech

KAPLAN PUBLI

Benefits

- There are two main categories:
  - (1) Exempt benefits
  - (2) Taxable benefits

Exempt benefits

- Trivial benefits (except vouchers) with a cost to the employer of less than £50 per gift and not in recognition of services provided
- Employer's contribution to registered pension scheme
- Canteen facilities provided for all employees
- Employee relocation costs up to £8,000
- Works buses for home to work travel
- Job-related accommodation
- One mobile telephone for private use per employee
- Workplace nurseries for childcare
- Payment for approved childcare up to limits of:
  - £55 per week (BR taxpayer),
  - £28 per week (HR taxpayer), or
  - £25 per week (AR taxpayer)

- Up to £4 per week (or £18 per month) towards additional household costs where the employee works from home
- Annual staff parties costing under £150 per person per annum
- Car parking space at or near place of work
- Reimbursement of expenses for working away from home:
  - £5 per night if in the UK, and
  - £10 per night if overseas
- Recreational or sporting facilities available to all employees and not to the public generally
- Cheap loans provided loan is ≤ £10,000 throughout the tax year
- Medical expenses of up to £500 per employee per tax year to enable an employee to return to work following an absence due to injury or ill health.

Key Point

Any exempt benefits should be:

- excluded in the employment income computation
- but noted as exempt in section C examination answers.

Taxable benefits

£

General principles

When calculating the taxable amount for any benefit consider:

- Payments made by the employee for the benefit = deductible

- Time apportionment when the benefit is only available for part of the tax year.

Benefit calculated for tax year	X
Less: Periods where unavailable	(X)
Less: Employee contributions	(X)
Taxable benefit	X

Benefit	Amount assessable
Cash vouchers	Cash which voucher can be exchanged for
Non-cash vouchers	Cost to employer
Credit cards	All items purchased for personal use (not interest or card charges)
Payment by employer of an employee's liability	Amount paid by employer (e.g. home telephone bill)
Living accommodation	Up to three components (see below)
Cars & fuel	Based on CO_2 emissions
Vans	Flat rate scale charge
Interest free/low interest loans	Based on official rate of interest
Assets loaned	Based on 20% of market value of asset when first provided
Gift of new asset	Cost to employer
Other	Cost to the employer, or Marginal cost to the employer for 'in-house' benefits

Living accommodation

Benefit	Amount assessable	Job-related accommodation
Basic charge	Higher of: • Annual value • Rent paid by employer	Exempt
Expensive accommodation charge (where employer owns property and cost is > £75,000)	(Cost – £75,000) x ORI ORI = official rate of interest (provided in the examination)	Exempt
Ancillary services:		
• Use of furniture	20% x market value when first provided	Same as for non-job related accommodation except: Maximum total benefit restricted to 10% of other employment income
• Living expenses (e.g. heating, electricity, decorating)	Cost to employer	
• Council tax	Cost to employer	No charge

Key Point

- Where the employer rents the accommodation there can never be an expensive accommodation charge.

- For the expensive accommodation charge:

  Cost = Acquisition cost of the property **plus** capital improvements up to the **start** of the tax year.

  If the property is occupied by the employee more than 6 years after it was acquired by the employer:

  – substitute the acquisition cost with the market value at the date the property was first occupied by the employee.

Job-related accommodation

Definition

Accommodation which is:

- necessary for proper performance of employee's duties, or

- provided for the better performance of duties and it is customary to provide such accommodation, or

- provided as part of special security arrangements because of a specific threat to the employee's security.

Exam focus

Exam kit questions in this area:

Constructed response (section C) questions

- Richard Tryer

Company cars

- Benefit arises where an employer provides a car and it is available for private use.
- Benefit:

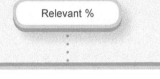

Relevant % x List price of car (when new)

- Based on CO_2 emissions (g/km)
- Cars with ≥ 95 g/km CO_2 emissions:
  16% (petrol) or 19% (diesel)
  + 1% for every 5 g/km over 95 g/km
- Cars with CO_2 emissions of 76 – 94 g/km:
  15% (petrol) or 18% (diesel)
- Cars with CO_2 emissions of 51 – 75 g/km:
  11% (petrol) or 14% (diesel)
- Cars with ≤ 50 g/km CO_2 emissions:
  7% (petrol) or 10% (diesel)
- 37% overall cap

- Include extras
- Reduced by employee contribution to capital cost (max £5,000)

- If car unavailable for part of the year:
  - Proportional reduction in benefit only if car unavailable for > 30 days.
- Employee contributions for private use
  - reduce taxable benefit.
- Cars only used for business (e.g. pool cars)
  - no taxable benefit.
- Car benefit figure includes all running costs of the car (i.e. there is no additional benefit for insurance, services, etc. paid for by the employer).

Exam focus

Exam kit questions in this area:

Constructed response (section C) questions

- Richard Feast
- Richard Tryer
- Samson and Delilah

Fuel benefit

- Where fuel provided for private use of a company car.
- Benefit:

Relevant % × £22,200

- Relevant % = same as car benefit
- No benefit if:
  - Employee pays for all fuel for private use.
  - Fuel is only provided for business use.
- If private fuel is permanently withdrawn the benefit is proportionately reduced.

Exam kit questions in this area:

Constructed response (section C) questions:

- Richard Tryer

There is no reduction in the fuel benefit where an employee only partially reimburses the cost of private fuel.

Company vans

- Flat rate scale charge of £3,170 p.a.
- Additional benefit of £598 p.a. if private fuel is provided.
- No benefit if private use is insignificant or limited to ordinary commuting between home and work.

Beneficial loans

Where an employee is provided with an interest free or cheap loan:

	£
Interest on outstanding balance at ORI	X
Less: Interest actually paid	(X)
Taxable benefit	X

ORI = official rate of interest
(will be given in the examination)

For FA2016 examination sittings, ORI = 3%

Exam focus

Exam kit questions in this area:

Constructed response (section C) questions:

- Patience
- Daniel, Francine and Gregor
- John Beach

Two methods of calculating of the benefit:

- Average method
- Precise method.

Average method

- Average balance for the year is calculated by:

$$\frac{L_1 + L_2}{2} \times \frac{M}{12}$$

  L_1 loan outstanding at the beginning of the tax year or date when first loaned if loaned during tax year

  L_2 loan outstanding at the end of the tax year or date fully repaid if repaid in full during tax year

  M Number of whole income tax months during which the loan was outstanding in the tax year.

Precise method

- ORI charged on a daily basis on the actual amount outstanding (calculated on monthly basis in the examination).
- Taxpayer or HMRC allowed to elect for the precise method to be used.

Exceptions

- No benefit if:
  - total of loans outstanding at any time in the tax year is ≤ £10,000, or
  - loans are made on ordinary commercial terms (i.e. same terms as to the public).

Exam focus

The benefit should be calculated using both methods in the examination unless the question states otherwise.

Use and transfer of assets

Use of asset

- 20% of market value of asset when first made available.
- 20% rule does not apply to private use of cars, vans and accommodation provided by an employer.

Transfer of asset

New asset

- Benefit = Cost to employer

Used asset:

- Benefit is greater of:

	£
– Market value at time of transfer	X
Less: Amount paid by employee	(X)
	X

  and

	£
– Market value when first used	X
Less: Amount charged as benefit over period of use	(X)
Less: Amount paid by employee	(X)
	X

- These rules do not apply to the transfer of:

  - a used car or van

  - bicycles provided for work.

  The benefit in this instance is the market value at the date of transfer.

chapter

3

Income from self-employment

In this chapter

- Badges of trade.
- Trading income.
- Adjustment of trading profit.
- Disallowable expenditure.
- Trading income not included in the accounts.
- Non-trading income.
- Expenditure not charged in the accounts but allowable trading expenditure.
- Cash basis for small businesses.
- Flat rate expense deduction.

Badges of trade

- Factors used to determine if an activity constitutes trading or an investment.
- The outcome of this decision will affect whether the income is taxed as a capital gain or trading income.
- Original six badges of trade:

Test		Consider
Subject matter	S	Is asset purchased for personal use, an investment or for trading? Some assets are more normally purchased for personal reasons/investment (e.g. painting) than for trading purposes (e.g. toilet rolls)
Ownership period	O	Brief period of ownership indicates trading
Frequency of transactions	F	Repeated similar transactions indicate trading
Improvements	I	Work to make asset more marketable may indicate trading
Reason for sale	R	Forced sale to raise cash indicates not trading
Motive	M	Intention to profit from transaction indicates trading

Also consider:

Test		Consider
Finance	F	Was a loan taken out to finance the purchase which will need to be repaid on sale?
Acquisition method	A	An asset acquired via a gift or inheritance indicates not trading
Existence of Similar Trading Transactions	S T	Similarities to an existing trade indicate trading

Key Point

Remember: SOFIRM and FAST

Be prepared to use the badges of trade to determine whether a particular transaction would be classed as a trading activity.

Trading income

The profits of an unincorporated trader arising from a trade are assessed as trading income.

To determine the assessable profits:

(1) Adjust the net profit per the accounts for tax purposes

(2) Apply the basis of assessment rules to determine the profits taxable in a tax year (Chapter 5).

Adjustment of trading profit

The starting point is the net profit per the business' financial accounts.

Need to adjust this figure for items that are disallowable for tax purposes and income that is not taxable as trading income.

Pro forma – Tax adjusted trading profit

	£	£
Net profit per accounts	X	
Add: Expenditure not allowed for taxation purposes	X	
Expenditure allowable for taxation purposes	0	
Taxable trading profit not credited in the accounts	X	
Less: Expenditure not charged in the accounts but allowable for the purposes of taxation		X
Income included in the accounts that is not taxable as trading profit		X
Capital allowances (see Chapter 4)		X
	X	Y
	(Y)	
Tax-adjusted trading profit	X	

The tax adjusted profit computation is a regularly tested topic for the F6 examination. It is essential that you learn the pro forma for adjusting trading profits and practise questions in this area.

Exam kit questions in this area:

OT case (section B) questions:

* Greenzone Ltd

Constructed response (section C) questions:

* Richard Feast
* Chi Needle
* E-Commerce plc
* Lucky Ltd
* Retro Ltd
* Jump Ltd
* Clueless Ltd
* Long Ltd and Road Ltd

Disallowable expenditure

* General rule:
  only expenditure incurred **wholly** and **exclusively** for the **purposes of the trade** is allowable.

* Adjust for proprietor's private expenditure.
  Examples:

  – Income tax payments

  – NICs

  – Private element of expenses such a[s] motoring expenses and telephone bills

* Disallow the proprietor's salary/drawing[s]

Salaries/private expenses of employees are allowable.

Disallowable expenditure – examples

Disallowable	Allowable
Capital expenditure	
Depreciation, profit/loss on sale of assets, improvements	Repairs
Legal fees	
If relate to capital item (e.g. purchase of a building) Exceptions: • costs of renewing short lease (≤ 50 years) • costs of defending title to an asset • cost of raising loan finance	If relate to revenue item (e.g. collection of trade receivables)
Fines/penalties	
VAT penalties, fine for breaking health & safety regulations	Parking fine incurred by employee (but not proprietor/owner)
Donations	
To national charities/political parties gift aid donations	Small amounts to local charities – effectively advertising

Disallowable	Allowable
Entertaining	
Customers, suppliers	Staff
Impairment losses	
Write off of non-trade debt (e.g. loan to a customer)	Write off of trade debt
	Allowance for impairment of trade receivables
Interest payable	
Late payment interest re overdue tax	Interest paid on trading loans (e.g. bank overdraft, hire purchase contracts)

Car leasing costs

Part of leasing/hire charge is disallowed for high emission cars (CO_2 emissions are more than 130 g/km).

Disallowed amount = (15% x leasing costs or hire charge).

Gifts to customers

Only allowable if:

- incorporates conspicuous advertisement for the business, and
- total cost per donee is < £50 per annum, and
- does not consist of food, drink or tobacco.

Gifts to staff

Allowable.

Trading income not included in the accounts

- Most common example is goods taken by proprietor for his own use.
- Trader treated as making a sale to himself at the normal selling price.
- If no entries have been made in the accounts for the transaction
  - add back the sale price.
- If the trader has already added back the cost of the goods in the accounts
  - only add back the profit element of the transaction.

Non-trading income

- Deduct income that is taxed in another way or is not taxable.
- This income is deducted from the net profit per the accounts.

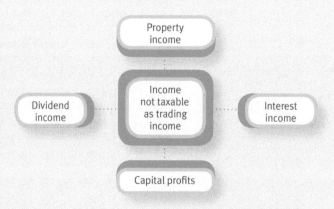

Expenditure not charged in the accounts but allowable trading expenditure

- Capital allowances.
- Any business expense paid for by the proprietor (e.g. business calls on a home telephone).
- The annual deduction for premium paid by tenant for grant of short lease on business premises:

$$\text{Deduction} = \frac{Y}{\text{Period of lease}}$$

Y = premium assessable on landlord as property income calculated as follows:

	£
Premium	X
Less: 2% x (n – 1) x premium	(X)
	Y

Where n = duration of lease in years

Alternative calculation:

$$P \times \left(\frac{51 - n}{50} \right)$$

It is highly likely that an adjustment of profit question will feature in your exam.

The presentation of the question is usually in the form of an extract from the statement of profit or loss, complete with notes and a breakdown of each of the different types of income and expense.

The way to tackle these questions is to carefully work through the scenario, making a note of any disallowable expenditure or non-trading income.

Make sure you don't forget to include the obvious adjustments, such as depreciation and capital allowances.

If you are in doubt as to how to treat a particular item, use the basic "wholly and exclusively" test.

If still in doubt, make an educated assumption of how to treat the item and state your assumption on your answer paper.

Then layout the pro forma, starting with the net profit figure, and systematically work through all the items of expenditure and income in the question, ticking them off as you go along.

By using the pro forma, and sticking to this logical approach, you will ensure you don't miss anything out of the question.

For section C questions, note that any allowable items must still be shown in your answer in the order they appear in the question, and shown as an add back adjustment of zero (0).

Similarly, all income should be listed and non-trading income adjusted for.

It is important to use the pro forma in section C questions to make your answer as clear a possible for the marker.

Cash basis for small businesses

- Cash basis = calculating profits/losses on the basis of cash received and cash paid in the period of account (instead of normal accruals basis).
- Optional.
- Only available to unincorporated businesses (e.g. sole traders and partnerships) – not companies and LLPs.
- Business must have annual turnover < VAT registration threshold (i.e. £83,000).
- Can continue to account on cash basis until annual turnover = 2 x VAT registration threshold (i.e. £166,000).

Exam focus

It should be assumed that the cash basis does **not** apply **unless** it is specifically mentioned in the question.

Under the cash basis:

- accounts can be prepared to any date in the year.
- there is no distinction between capital and revenue expenditure re plant, machinery and equipment for tax purposes;
- the flat rate expense deduction for car expenses (see below) will always be claimed instead of capital allowances in the F6 examination.

Advantages

- Simpler accounting.
- Profit taxed when realised and cash available to pay.

Disadvantages

- Losses can only be carried forward.

Flat rate expense deduction

Any unincorporated business (whether or not they are using the cash basis) can:

- opt to use flat rate expense adjustments
- to replace the calculation of actual costs incurred in respect of those expenses.

Exam focus

However in the F6 examination:

- flat rate expenses will only be examined where the business has chosen the cash basis, and
- if the cash basis applies, the use of flat rate expenses will be assumed to also apply.

Calculate the profit under the cash basis by doing a revised profit computation, rather than adjusting the net profit (as you would under the accruals basis).

Type of expense	Flat rate expense adjustment
Motoring expenses	Allowable deduction = amount using the AMAP rates of 45p and 25p per mile (Note 1)
Private use of part of a commercial building (e.g. accommodation in a small hotel or guest house)	Adjustment = fixed amount based on the number of occupants (Note 2). Covers: private use of household goods and services, rent, food and utilities

Notes: If required:

1. AMAP rates are included in the tax rates and allowances provided to you in the examination.

2. Fixed amount will be provided within the question.

Private element of other expenses (e.g. council tax and rates) = adjusted for as norm

4

Sole trader: capital allowances

In this chapter

Introduction

- Depreciation is disallowable for tax purposes.

- Tax relief for capital expenditure on certain types of expenditure (i.e. plant and machinery) is given through capital allowances.

- Capital allowances are:

  - Calculated for a trader's period of account.

  - Deductible from adjusted trading profits.

Plant and machinery

Definition

Plant and Machinery (P&M)

'Plant' is an item **with which** the trade is carried on (active function) and not the setting **in which** it is carried on (passive function).

```
                  Function

       Active                    Passive
  Apparatus with              Setting in
  which business            which business
   carried on                 carried on
```

Examples of plant and machinery

- Computers and software
- Machinery
- Cars and lorries
- Office furniture
- Movable partitions
- Air-conditioning
- Alterations of buildings to install plant and machinery

Expenditure which is not 'plant and machinery'

- False ceilings (part of the building).
- Fixed partitions.

Pro forma – Capital allowances computation

	£	Main pool £	Special rate pool £	Short life asset £	Private use asset £	Allowances £
TWDV b/f		X	X	X		
Additions not qualifying for AIA or FYA:						
Second-hand low emission cars (up to 75 g/km)		X				
Cars (76–130 g/km)		X				
Cars (over 130 g/km)			X			
Car with private use					X	
Additions qualifying for AIA:						
Special rate pool expenditure	X					
Less: AIA (Max £200,000 in total)	(X)					X
Transfer balance to special rate pool			X			
Plant and machinery	X					
Less: AIA (Max £200,000 in total)	(X)					X
Transfer balance to main pool		X				
Disposals (lower of original cost and sale proceeds)		(X)		(X)		
		X	X	X	X	X

	£	Main pool £	Special rate pool £	Short life asset £	Private use asset £	Allowances £
BA / (BC)				(X) / X		X / (X)
Small pools WDA						
WDA at 18%		(X)				X
WDA at 8%			(X)			X
WDA at 8%/18% (depending on emissions)					(X) × BU%	X
Additions qualifying for FYAs:						
New low emission cars (up to 75 g/km)	X					
Less: FYA at 100%	(X)					X
	—	0				
TWDV c/f		X	X		X	
Total allowances						X

Sole trader: capital allowances

Vans, lorries and motorbikes are treated like plant and machinery and not like motor cars.

It is essential that you learn this capital allowances pro forma in order to present your calculations in a structured manner.

Note that the main pool can also be referred to as the general pool.

Exam kit questions in this area:

OT case (section B) questions:

- Greenzone Ltd

Constructed response (section C) questions

- John and Lian
- Richard Feast
- Chi Needle
- Alfred King
- Jump Ltd
- Softapp Ltd
- E-Commerce plc
- Lucky Ltd
- Clueless Ltd
- Long Ltd and Road Ltd

The allowances

The Annual Investment Allowance (AIA)

- Available to all businesses.
- 100% allowance for £200,000 of expenditure incurred in each accounting period of 12 months.
- Applied pro rata for periods of account that are not 12 months.
- Available on acquisitions in the order:
  - special rata pool items
  - plant and machinery in main pool
  - short life assets
  - private use assets.
- **Not** available on cars.
- Not available in the accounting period in which trade ceases.
- Expenditure above the maximum qualifies for a WDA immediately.

- Taxpayer does not have to claim all / any of the AIA if he does not want to.
- Any unused AIA is lost.

Writing Down Allowances (WDA)

- Available to all businesses.
- WDA available on a reducing balance basis.
- 18% in all pools except the special rate pool.
- Special rate pool WDA = 8%.
- Applied pro rata for periods of account that are not 12 months.
- WDA adjusted for assets with private use by owner of business.

AN PUBLISHING

59

First year allowances (FYA)

- Available to all businesses.
- 100% FYA available on:
  - new low emission cars
    ($CO_2 \leq 75$ g/km)
    (not available on any other cars).
- Only available in the period of acquisition.
- Never time apportion for short or long accounting periods.
- Taxpayer does not have to claim all/any of the FYA if he does not want to.
- If any of the FYA is not claimed:
  - the balance is put in the main pool
  - but not entitled to WDA until the following period.

Balancing adjustments

- Assets disposed of:
  - Deduct the sale proceeds from the relevant pool.
  - The amount deducted can never exceed the original cost of the asset
  - A balancing adjustment may arise.

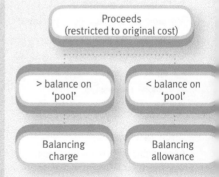

- A balancing charge (BC):
  - Can occur on any pool at any time.

- A balancing allowance (BA):
  - Can occur on a 'single asset' column at any time.
  - Only occurs on main pool or special rate pool when the business ceases to trade.

Summary of the capital allowances available for cars

CO_2 emissions

• Low emission cars:
  – Emissions ≤ 75 g/km
  – New = FYA 100%
  – Secondhand = as for standard emission cars

• Standard emission cars:
  – Emissions 76 – 130 g/km
  – Put in main pool
  – WDA 18% for 12 month period

• High emission cars:
  – Emissions >130 g/km
  – Put in special rate pool
  – WDA 8% for 12 month period

• Private use cars:
  – Separate column
  – WDA 18%/8% for 12 month period depending on emissions
  – BA or BC will arise on disposal

The special rate pool

- Pool expenditure incurred on:
  - long life assets (LLA)
  - integral features of a building
  - thermal insulation of a building
  - high emission cars (CO_2 >130 g/km).
- Pool operates in the same way as the main pool.
- AIA is available on new expenditure in this pool (except high emission cars).
- AIA given against new expenditure in this pool first.
- WDA = 8% for a 12 month period, reducing balance basis.
- FYA are never available.
- LLA = assets
  - with a working life ≥ 25 years, and
  - expenditure incurred ≥ £100,000 for a 12 month period (but not cars or P&M in a retail shop, showroom, hotel or office).

- Integral features
  = expenditure incurred on:
  - electrical (including lighting) systems
  - cold water systems
  - space or water heating systems
  - external solar shading
  - powered systems of ventilation, air cooling or air purification
  - lifts, escalators and moving walkways
- Thermal insulation of a building
  = expenditure on thermal insulation on any commercial building (exception = residential buildings in a property business).

The small pool WDA

- Applies to the main pool and special rate pool only
    - can claim on either or both pools
    - claim is optional.
- Available where the balance on the pool after current period additions and disposals is ≤ £1,000.
- WDA = any amount up to £1,000 for a 12 month period.
- Applied pro rata if period of account is not 12 months.

Short life assets (SLA)

- Each short life asset has its own column.
- Short life means there is intention to sell/scrap the asset within 8 years of end of POA acquired.
- AIA available.
- A balancing allowance/charge will arise when the asset is disposed of.
- Beneficial where asset with a short life is to be disposed of for less than its TWDV.
- Not available for motor cars.
- If the asset is not disposed of within 8 years after the end of the period of account in which it was acquired
    - the TWDV is transferred to the main pool.
- Election required for SLA treatment:
    - by first anniversary of 31 January following the end of the tax year in which the trading period, in which the asset was acquired, ends.

Private use assets (Unincorporated businesses only)

- Separate column for each private use asset.
- Pool is:
  - written down by the AIA/WDA in full, according to the length of the accounting period, or FYA
  - but actual allowance claimed is restricted to business use proportion.
- BC/BA on disposal is also restricted to business use proportion.
- Cannot claim SLA treatment.
- Not applicable for companies.

Business cessation

- Additions and disposals are allocated to relevant pools.
- No AIAs, WDAs or FYAs are given.
- Balancing adjustments arise on each pool and bring the TWDV down to nil:
  - TWDV positive = allowance given.
  - TWDV negative = charge arises.

Approach to computational questions

For P&M capital allowances, adopt the following step-by-step approach:

(1) Read the information in the question and decide how many columns / pools you will require.

(2) Draft the layout and insert the TWDV b/f (does not apply in a new trade).

(3) Insert additions not eligible for the AIA or FYAs into the appropriate column taking care to allocate cars into the correct column according to CO_2 emissions.

(4) Insert additions eligible for the AIA in the first column, then allocate the AIA to the additions.

Remember to time apportion if the period of account is not 12 months.

Allocate the AIA to special rate pool additions in priority to additions of P&M in the main or other individual asset pools.

(5) Any special rate pool additions in excess of the AIA must be added to the special rate pool to increase the balance available for 8% WDA.

Any main pool expenditure in excess of the AIA should be added to the main pool to increase the balance qualifying for 18% WDA.

(6) Deal with any disposal by deducting the lower of cost and sale proceeds.

(7) Work out any balancing charge / balancing allowance for assets in individual columns.

Remember to adjust for any private use if an unincorporated business (not relevant for companies).

(8) Consider if the small pools WDA applies to the main pool and / or the special rate pool.

(9) Calculate the WDA on each of the pools at the appropriate rate (18% or 8%).

Remember to:

- time apportion if the period of account is not 12 months

- adjust for any private use if an unincorporated business (not relevant for companies).

(10) Insert any additions of new cars with emissions of 75 g/km or less, which will get 100% FYA.

Remember the FYA is never time apportioned.

(11) Calculate the TWDV to carry forward to the next accounting period and add the allowances column.

(12) Deduct the total allowances from the tax adjusted trading profits.

Be aware of scenarios in the exam where the question asks for a computation of both an adjustment of profits and capital allowances

Sometimes the information listed within the repairs and renewal 'notes to the accounts' could include items that should be classed as plant & machinery.

Remember to:

- disallow these items in your adjustment of profits as they are capital expenditure, but

- include them within your P&M capital allowance workings.

For example, a replacement printer could be included as a 'repair' in the statement of profit or loss. This should be disallowed in the adjustment of profits as it is a new capital item, but qualifies for AIA and WDA as P&M in the main pool.

Length of the accounting period

- The AIA and WDA are given for a 12 month period.
- If the period of account is less than 12 months:
  - scale down AIA and WDA
  - applies to both individuals and companies.
- If the period of account exceeds 12 months:

  For individuals:
  - scale up AIA and WDA

  For companies:
  - split period into two chargeable accounting periods (CAP), if a company (Chapter 14), because a CAP cannot exceed 12 months
  - remember that the second CAP will be less than 12 months; therefore the AIA and WDA will be scaled down in that CAP.

Key Point

FYAs are always given in full regardless of the length of the period of account.

5

Sole trader: basis of assessment

In this chapter

- Basis of assessment.
- New businesses – opening year rules.
- Overlap profits.
- Business ceases – closing year rules.

Basis of assessment

Current year basis (CYB)

General rule:

Assessable trading income for a tax year
= the tax adjusted trading profit
   for the 12 month period of account
   ending in that tax year.

For example:

Accounts for the year ended 31 December
2016 = assessed in the tax year 2016/17.

New businesses – opening year rules

- Special rules to ensure there is an assessment for every tax year in which the business trades.

Tax year	Basis of assessment
First tax year (tax year in which trade starts)	Profits from date of commencement to following 5 April (Actual basis)
Second tax year (a) Period of account ending in the tax year is:	
(i) a 12 month period of account	That period of account (CYB)
(ii) less than 12 months long	The first twelve months of trading
(iii) more than 12 months long	Twelve months ending on the accounting date in the second tax year (i.e. the last 12 months of the long period of account)
(b) No period of account ending in the tax year	Actual profits from 6 April to 5 April
Third tax year	Twelve months ending on accounting date in the third tax year (usually CYB, but if a long period of account = the last 12 months of that long period)
Fourth year onwards	Normal CYB

Overlap profits

- Arise when profits are assessed more than once.
- Deducted from the final assessment when an individual ceases to trade.

Exam focus

Exam kit questions in this area:

Constructed response (section C) questions:

- John and Lian
- Fang, Hong and Kang

Business ceases – closing year rules

- Where an individual ceases to trade, any profits not yet assessed will be taxed in the tax year in which trading ceases.
- Penultimate tax year:
  - CYB.
- Final year:
  - Actual profit
    from the end of the basis period of the penultimate year of assessment to date of cessation.
  - Deduct any unrelieved overlap profits.

Key Point

Over the life of the business the profits assessed to tax will equal the taxable profits earned by the business.

6

Partnerships

In this chapter

- Introduction.
- Basis of assessment.
- Trading income assessments.
- Partnership losses.
- Limited liability partnerships (LLP).

Introduction

- A partnership is an unincorporated business but is not a separate legal entity; it is a collection of individuals working in business together.
- The partnership itself is not taxed.
- Each partner is responsible for their own tax liability arising from the partnership.
- Each partner pays income tax on his share of the trading profit of the business.

Basis of assessment

- The partnership accounting profit is adjusted in the same way as a sole trader.
- Capital allowances are claimed by the partnership, including those on the partners' own assets (e.g. cars).

  They are deducted from the adjusted trading profits to arrive at the tax adjusting trading profit of the partnership in the usual way.
- Each partner is assessed on his share of the partnership tax adjusted trading profits as if he were a sole trader (i.e. normally current year basis).

Trading income assessments

Treat like sole traders – each partner is the owner of the business.

Step 1	Determine the tax adjusted accounting profit/loss after capital allowances of the partnership for each accounting period.
Step 2	Allocate these profits or losses between the partners according to the **profit sharing agreement** (PSA) in the **accounting period**.
	If PSA requires a salary or interest on capital allocation:
	• treat as a share of the trading profits.
	The balance of profits or losses:
	• shared in the profit sharing ratio (PSR).
	If a partner joins or leaves during the accounting period:
	• treat as if a change in PSR
	• time apportion profits, apply appropriate PSA to each part.
Step 3	Determine the taxable trading income assessment for the tax year or the loss reliefs available for each partner using their share of the accounting profit/loss.
	Partner joins – opening year rules
	Partner leaves – closing year rules
	Other years – normal CYB basis (i.e. assess the profits of 12 months to a/c date)

Key Point

PSAs may allocate salaries and/or interest on fixed capital. These are taxed as trading profits and not salary or interest income.

They are allocated to the partners first and then any remaining balance of partnership profits is allocated according to the partnership profit sharing ratio (PSR).

Key Point

When a partner joins/leaves a partnership, the special opening/closing year rules only apply to the partner joining or leaving the partnership.

Continuing partners will continue to be assessed on the CYB.

Exam focus

Exam kit questions in this area:

Constructed response (section C) questions:

*   Samson and Delilah

Exam focus

Exam kit questions in this area:

Constructed response (section C) questions:

*   Fang, Hong and Kang
*   Alfred King
*   Daniel, Francine and Gregor

Partnership losses

- Partnership losses are calculated and allocated between the partners in the same way as profits.
- Each partner may claim loss relief under the normal rules.
- Only partners joining the partnership are eligible for special opening years carry back relief.
- Only partners leaving the partnership are eligible for terminal loss relief.

Limited liability partnerships (LLP)

- An LLP is a special type of partnership where the amount that each partner may be required to contribute towards the partnership losses, debts and liabilities is limited by agreement.
- For F6, they are taxed in the same way as other partnerships.

7

Individuals: relief for trading losses

In this chapter

- Ongoing businesses.
- Opening years relief.
- Terminal loss relief.
- Maximum deduction from total income.
- Procedure for dealing with loss questions.
- Choice of loss reliefs.

Ongoing businesses

Trading losses
- Calculated in the same way as a trading profit.
- Trading income assessment is nil.

Relief against total income
- Available in:
  - tax year of the loss and/or;
  - preceding tax year

- Offset cannot be restricted to preserve PA.
- Offset is restricted if loss exceeds maximum amount (see below).
- Excess loss is automatically carried forward or can be set against chargeable gains.

Relief against chargeable gains
- Available in the same years as a claim against total income:
  - tax year of the loss, and/or
  - preceding tax year.
- Only possible after a claim against total income has been made in the tax year in which a claim against gains is required.
- Do not need to claim against total income in both years first
- No maximum restriction.

Relief against future trading profits
- Relieved against:
  - the first available
  - trading profits only
  - of the same trade.
- Loss offset cannot be restricted.

- Trading loss is treated as a current year capital loss
- Deducted
  - after the offset of current year capital losses
  - before capital losses brought forward, and
  - before the AEA.

The exam could require you to identify all the options available before deciding how to offset the loss.

Order of offset

When there is more than one loss to offset:

- deal with the earliest loss first
- losses b/f are offset in priority to CY and PY claims.
- watch out for the maximum restriction (if applicable) (see below).

Exam kit questions in this area:

Constructed response (section C) questions:

- Fang, Hong and Kang
- Michael and Sean
- Daniel, Francine and Gregor

Opening years relief

In addition to reliefs available for an ongoing business, special opening year loss relief is available.

- A loss incurred in any of the **first four tax years** of a new business can be set against:
  - total income
  - of the three tax years preceding the year of the loss
  - on a FIFO basis.
- One claim covers all three years.
- Offset cannot be restricted to preserve PA.
- Maximum restriction applies as for ongoing loss relief against total income.

Exam kit questions in this area:

Constructed response (section C) questions

- Michael and Sean

Terminal loss relief

In addition to standard relief against total income and chargeable gains, special terminal loss relief is available.

Relief is given for the loss of the **last 12 months** of trading.

- Relief is:
  - against profits of the same trade
  - of the tax year of cessation, and
  - the three preceding tax years
  - on a LIFO basis.
- Calculation of the terminal loss:
  - (1) loss from 6 April to date of cessation
  - (2) plus proportion of loss in the preceding tax year up to 12 months prior to cessation date
  - (3) plus unrelieved overlap profits.

Exam focus

Exam kit questions in this area:

Constructed response (section C) questions:

- Michael and Sean

Maximum deduction from total income

Maximum deduction from total income
= **greater of**:

- £50,000, or
- 25% of adjusted total income (ATI).

Therefore restriction will be £50,000 unless ATI exceeds £200,000.

Adjusted total income (ATI):

	£
Total income	X
Less: Gross PPCs	(X)
ATI	X

Key Point

The maximum restriction may be beneficial as it could avoid wasting PAs.

Maximum deduction limit:

- applies to trading losses set against:
  - current year total income
  - earlier years if set against income other than profits of the same trade.
- does not apply to losses set against chargeable gains.

Offset against earlier years:

- set against profits from same trade first, then non-trading income
- no restriction to offset against profits from same trade
- restrict offset against non-trading income
- loss that cannot be set off = not lost
  - can claim to offset against chargeable gains, or
  - c/f as usual.

Procedure for dealing with loss questions

(1) Determine tax adjusted loss/profits after capital allowances for each period of account.

(2) Determine when loss relief is available (i.e. in which tax years).

- Different options if in opening/ ongoing/ closing years.

(3) Layout IT computations for tax years side by side

- Leave spaces to insert losses offset.

(4) Set up a loss working for each loss to show how it is utilised.

(5) If more than one loss

- Consider in chronological order.

(6) Consider options available depending on whether early years of business, last year of business, chargeable gains in tax year.

(7) Offset losses in most beneficial way or as instructed by the question requirement

- Watch out for maximum restriction rules.

Choice of loss reliefs

- To choose the most appropriate claim:
    - obtain relief at the highest marginal tax rate
    - obtain relief as early as possible
    - avoid wasting PAs (and the AEA for CGT where appropriate).
- Relief against total income and special opening year relief give earliest relief, rather than carry forward loss relief.
- A large gain in a single year (the year of loss or year immediately preceding):
    - indicates that a claim against chargeable gains may be beneficial
    - but must relieve total income of same year first and maximum restriction may apply
    - may result in wastage of PAs
    - maximum restriction does not apply against gains

- relief against gains is at 10% or 20% depending on the taxpayer's remaining basic rate band (18% or 28% if the gain resulted from the disposal of residential property).
- Relief against total income and special opening year relief are optional but carrying forward the loss is mandatory and automatic if no specific claim is made.
- No partial claims allowed (i.e. all or nothing reliefs).
- Relief against total income applies to two years but separate claims are required for each year and such claims can be made in either order.
- The best claim may be a compromise of the main objectives (e.g. may accept lower tax saving if relief is given earlier)

Pensions and national insurance contributions

In this chapter

- Pension contributions.
- National insurance contributions (NICs).
- Employees.
- Employers.
- Self-employed individuals.

Pension contributions

Types of pension scheme:

- Occupational pension schemes (set up by employers for their employees)
- Personal pension schemes (available to any individual).

Exam focus

Exam kit questions in this area:

OT case (section B) questions:

- Philip and Charles

Constructed response (section C) questions:

- Patience
- Richard Tryer
- John Beach
- Rosie and Tom

Tax relief for pension contributions:

- Any amount can be contributed by an individual into any number of pension schemes, but **tax relief** is only available on a **maximum amount** each year.

- Tax relief available on contributions up to the **lower** of:

  (a) Total gross contributions paid

  (b) Maximum amount = higher of:

     (i) £3,600 and

     (ii) 100% x (relevant earnings).

- Relevant earnings:

  - trading profits

  - employment income

  - furnished holiday letting income.

- An individual with no relevant earnings can therefore obtain tax relief on contributions of up to £3,600 per year.

Method of giving tax relief

Employee contributions

Pension contribution to:

Personal pension scheme

Occupational scheme

- Basic rate relief (20%) given at source.
- Higher rate relief given by extending basic rate band.
- Additional rate relief given by extending higher rate band.

Tax relief at all rates given at source through PAYE system (i.e. an allowable deduction against employment income).

Employer contributions

- Not treated as a taxable benefit.
- Tax deductible for employer.
- Taken into account when calculating total contributions to be compared with annual allowance (AA).

Annual Allowance (AA)

- Where total contributions paid into pension schemes > the current year AA plus unused AA b/f:
  - a tax charge arises on the excess.
- The tax charge is:
  - taxed as the individual's top slice of income.
  - paid through the self-assessment system.

Exam focus

In the examination:

- add the excess to the taxpayer's total income, and
- tax that part last (i.e. after dividends).

- Unused AA b/f from the **previous three tax years** is taken into account:
  - can only be c/f if the individual was a member of a registered pension scheme for that tax year.
- The AA for the 3 years prior to 2016/17 was:
  - 2015/16: £40,000
  - 2014/15: £40,000
  - 2013/14: £50,000
- Order of utilisation:
  - current year AA is used first
  - then earlier three years unused amount, on a FIFO basis.

Restriction of annual allowance – high income individuals

- The annual allowance is gradually reduced for individuals with high income

- The restriction applies to individuals with 'adjusted income' exceeding £150,000.
- The annual allowance is reduced by:
  (Adjusted income − £150,000) × 50%
- The maximum reduction to the annual allowance is £30,000, which means the minimum annual allowance will be £10,000.

Adjusted income	£
Net income (from the income tax computation)	x
Plus: Individual **employee's occupational pension** contributions	x
Employer's contributions into any scheme for that individual	x
Adjusted income	x

Accessing the pension fund

- Minimum age for accessing pension fund is 55.
- Defined benefit schemes:
  - benefits linked to the level of earnings of the employee.
- Money purchase schemes:
  - Benefits dependent on the amount of funds accumulated in the pension fund (i.e. contributions plus investment income/gains).
  - Can withdraw 25% of the fund as a tax free lump sum.
  - Balance (remaining 75%) of the fund, can be accessed in a variety of ways.
  - Withdrawals from the balance of the fund are taxed as non-savings income in the tax year they are withdrawn at the normal rates of tax (i.e. 20%, 40% or 45%).

Lifetime Allowance (LA)

- LA = Total pension value that can obtain tax relief.
- LA for 2016/17 is £1,000,000.
- Considered when an individual becomes entitled to take benefits out of the pension scheme (e.g. he becomes entitled to a pension).
- If the value of the pension fund at that time exceeds the LA; an additional tax charge arises.
- Calculation of this tax charge is not examinable.

National insurance contributions (NICs)

- Different classes of NICs are paid depending on the individual's status.

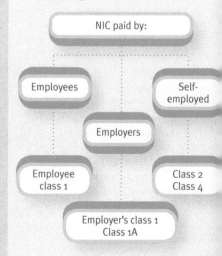

NIC paid by:

Employees

Self-employed

Employers

Employee class 1

Class 2
Class 4

Employer's class 1
Class 1A

Employees

Employee class 1

- Employees pay class 1 NICs on their 'cash earnings'.
- Cash earnings includes:
  - any remuneration derived from employment and paid in money
  - vouchers exchangeable for cash or goods
  - reimbursement of cost of travel between home and work.
- Cash earnings does not include:
  - exempt employment benefits
  - most non-cash benefits
  - reimbursement of business expenses.
  - mileage allowance up to 45p per mile.
- Payable by all employees aged 16 to state pension age.

- Payable at 12% on earnings between £8,060 and £43,000.
- Payable at 2% on earnings above £43,000.
- Contributions are collected by the employer through the PAYE scheme.

Exam focus

Exam kit questions in this area:

Constructed response (section C) questions:

- George
- Sophia Wong
- John Beach
- Richard Feast
- Alfred King

Employers

- Employers
  - Employer's class 1
    - Cash earnings
      - Employment allowance
  - Class 1A
    - Benefits

Employer's class 1

- Cost borne by employer.
- Allowable trading expense for tax purposes.
- Rate of 13.8% on earnings over £8,112 per annum.
  - Note: no upper limit.
- Paid on 'cash earnings', as for employee class 1.
- Paid in respect of employees aged ≥ 16
  - Note: no upper limit.
- Employment allowance available.
- Payable with employer's class 1 contributions through PAYE system.
- Payable on 22 of the next month (electronic payments), or 19 of the next month if not paid electronically.

Exam focus

The electronic payday should be quoted in the examination as most businesses pay electronically.

Employment allowance

- Up to £3,000 p.a. allowance
- Deducted from employer's class 1 NICs only.
- Claimed though the RTI PAYE system.

Class 1A

- Payable by the employer only.
- Rate of 13.8% on taxable benefits provided to the employee.
- Payable by 22 July following the tax year (if paid electronically) or 19 July (if not paid electronically).

Exam focus

Exam kit questions in this area:
Constructed response (section C) questions:

- Richard Feast
- John Beach

Self-employed individuals

Self-employed

Class 2
- Fixed at £2.80 per week.
- Paid at the same time as the balancing payment for income tax under self-assessment.

Class 4
- Paid on taxable trade profits less losses b/f.
- Rate of 9% on profits which fall between £8,060 and £43,000.
- Rate of 2% on profits which exceed £43,000.
- Paid at the same time as income tax under self-assessment.
- Not payable if over state pension age or under 16 at the **start** of the tax year.

Key Point

Self-employed individuals who have employees pay:

- Class 2 and class 4 NICs in respect of their unincorporated trade, and

- Employer's class 1 and class 1A NICs in respect of earnings and benefits provided to employees.

Exam focus

Exam kit questions in this area:
Constructed response (section C) questions

- Alfred King

- Chi Needle

9

Ethics and income tax administration

In this chapter

- Professional Code of Ethics.
- Self-assessment.
- Records.
- Payment of income tax and class 4 NICs.
- Payment of class 2 NICs.
- Payment of capital gains tax.
- Interest.
- Claims.
- Penalties.
- HMRC compliance checks.
- Discovery assessments.
- Appeals.
- PAYE.

Professional Code of Ethics

Principles

- **O**bjectivity
- **P**rofessional behaviour
- **P**rofessional competence and due care
- **I**ntegrity
- **C**onfidentiality.

Key Point

Remember: OPPIC.

Exam focus

All of the topics in this chapter (ethics and tax administration) could be tested easily objective test questions in the F6 examination.

Exam kit questions in this area:

Constructed response (section C) questions

- Richard Feast

Tax evasion versus tax avoidance

- Tax evasion
  - unlawful
  - e.g. suppressing information or submitting false information
  - client = subject to criminal prosecution / fines / imprisonment
  - adviser = subject to sanctions of criminal law.

- Tax avoidance
  - use of the taxation system to legitimately reduce tax
  - e.g. advice to reduce tax liability
  - also used to describe tax schemes devised to utilise loopholes in the tax legislation.

- Specific schemes have been targeted with anti-avoidance legislation.

- HMRC have also introduced:
  - Disclosure obligations re specific tax avoidance schemes.
  - A general anti-abuse rule (GAAR) to counter artificial and abusive schemes to avoid tax. This targets arrangements which cannot be regarded as a reasonable course of action.

Dealing with HMRC

- Information provided must be accurate and complete.
- Must not assist a client to plan or commit an offence.
- If become aware of a tax irregularity:
  - discuss with client
  - ensure proper disclosure to HMRC.

- Client error
  - decide whether genuine or deliberate / fraudulent act
  - explain to client the need to notify HMRC
  - prompt / adequate disclosure taken into account when deciding penalties
  - if client refuses
    - must explain potential consequences in writing
    - if material, consider whether to continue to act for client
  - if client still refuses
    - should cease to act and write to HMRC stating that the firm no longer acts for the client but not stating the reason why.

Money laundering regulations

Money laundering = benefiting from or
concealing the proceeds of crime

- includes the proceeds of tax evasion.

A member of ACCA must appoint a Money
Laundering Reporting Officer (MLRO):

- decides whether to report a
  transaction to the National Crime
  Agency (NCA)
- if a report is made, client should not
  be informed as this is an offence
  (known as 'tipping off').

Dishonest conduct of tax agents

- Incurs a civil penalty of up to £50,000.
- HMRC may:
  - publish penalised tax agent's details
  - access working papers of a
    dishonest agent.

Self-assessment

Filing for 2016/17 returns

- Later of:
    - 31 October 2017 (paper return).
    - 31 January 2018 (electronic return).
    - Three months after the issue of the notice to file a return.
- Fixed and tax geared penalties may apply for late filing (see later).

Notification of chargeability

- Must notify HMRC of income or chargeable gains on which tax is due:
    - within six months from the end of the tax year in which the liability arises
    - i.e. by 5 October 2017 for 2016/17.
- standard penalty may arise for failure to notify chargeability (see later).

Exam focus

Exam kit questions in this area:
Constructed response (section C) questions:

- Richard Feast

Amendments to the return

- HMRC can amend return < 9 months of the actual filing date.
- Taxpayer can amend < 12 months of the 31 January filing date.

Determination of tax

- Issued by HMRC when a return is not filed by the 31 January filing date.
- Can be issued by HMRC within 3 years from the filing date (i.e. by 31 January 2021 for 2016/17 tax return).
- Assessment = replaced by the actual self-assessment return when it is submitted.

Records

Business records

- A business must keep records of:
  - all receipts and expenses
  - all goods purchased and sold
  - all supporting documents relating to the transactions of the business, such as accounts, books, contracts, vouchers and receipts.
- Self-employed taxpayers must retain all their records (not just business records) for five years after the 31 January following the end of the tax year.

  For 2016/17 = until 31 January 2023.

Other records

- Other taxpayers should keep evidence of income received.
- Must normally be retained for 12 months after the 31 January following the end of the tax year.

  For 2016/17 = until 31 January 2019.

Penalty

- A fixed penalty of up to £3,000 may be charged for failure to keep or retain adequate records.

Payment of income tax and class 4 NICs

Income tax and class 4 NICs are due as follows:

- 2 equal payments on account (POA):
  - 31 January in the tax year (31.1.17 for 2016/17)
  - 31 July after tax year (31.7.17 for 2016/17).

- Balancing payment due:
  - 31 January after the tax year (31.1.18 for 2016/17).

- Each POA is 50% of the previous year's income tax and class 4 NICs liability after the deduction of PAYE (= the relevant amount).

- POAs are not required if:
  - the relevant amount for the previous year is < £1,000, or
  - more than 80% of the income tax liability for the previous year was me by deduction of tax at source.

Exam focus

Exam kit questions in this area:

Constructed response (section C) questions

- Alfred King
- Sophia Shape
- George

Claims to reduce POAs

- At any time before 31 January following the tax year, a taxpayer can claim to reduce the POAs.
- Should only claim to reduce POAs if the tax liability (net of PAYE) for the current year is expected to be less than the POAs, based on the previous year's tax liability.
- An incorrect claim can lead to interest and penalties.

Payment of class 2 NICs

Class 2 NICs are payable under the self assessment system and are due by:

- 31 January after the tax year (31.1.2018 for 2016/17)
- POAs are not made for class 2 NIC.

Payment of capital gains tax

- CGT is payable under the self-assessment system and is due by:
  - 31 January following the tax year (31.1.2018 for 2016/17)
  - POAs are not made for CGT.

Exam focus

Exam kit questions in this area:

Constructed response (section C) questions:

- Sophia Shape

Interest

Late payment interest

Charged on:

- all late payments of tax
- at a daily rate
- runs from: due date
- to: date of payment.

Exam focus

All calculations in the examination will be to the nearest month unless the question states otherwise.

Repayment interest

HMRC pay interest on any overpaid tax

- from: later of
  - date tax due, or
  - date HMRC received tax
- to: date of repayment.

Interest on excessive claims to reduce POAs

- The interest charge is based on the difference between:
  - the amount actually paid, and
  - the amount that should have been paid.
- The amount that should have been paid = the lower of:
  - the original POAs based on the relevant amount for the previous year, and
  - 50% of the final tax liability (net of tax deducted at source) for the current year.
- Interest runs:
  - from: the due dates of
    - 31 January in the tax year and
    - 31 July following the tax year
  - to: the date of payment.

Claims

- Claims are usually made in the self-assessment return and must be quantified at the time of the claim.
- A claim which affects an earlier year (e.g. loss carry back), does not amend the earlier year but the tax saving is calculated as if the earlier year is amended.
- Carry back claims do not therefore reduce POAs for the year following the earlier year.
- The taxpayer can make a claim for overpayment relief to reduce tax within four years following the tax year concerned. A claim can be made in respect of errors made and mistakes arising from not understanding the law.

Penalties

Standard penalties

Applies in two circumstances:

- Submission of incorrect returns:
  - All taxes.
- Failure to notify liability to tax:
  - Income tax, CGT, corporation tax, VAT and NIC.
- Penalty = % of potential lost revenue.
- Depends on the behaviour of the taxpayer.

Taxpayer behaviour	Maximum penalty (% of revenue lost)
Genuine mistake (for incorrect returns only)	No penalty
Careless / Failure to take reasonable care	30%
Deliberate but no concealment	70%
Deliberate with concealment	100%

- Penalties may be reduced at HMRC discretion where the taxpayer informs HMRC
    - larger reductions for unprompted disclosure.
- Minimum penalties apply and vary based on:
    - the taxpayer's behaviour, and
    - whether disclosure is prompted or unprompted.
- An unprompted disclosure = where the taxpayer informs the HMRC when they had no reason to believe HMRC have or are about to discover the error.
- Taxpayer can appeal against a standard penalty.

Other penalties relating to individuals

Offence	Penalty
Late filing of self-assessment tax return	
– filed after due date	£100 fixed penalty
Additional penalties:	
– filed 3 months late	Daily penalties of £10 per day (maximum of 90 days) in addition to £100 fixed penalty
– filed 6 months late	5% of tax due (minimum £300) plus above penalties
– more than 12 months after filing date where withholding information was:	The penalties above plus:
– not deliberate	Additional 5% of tax due (minimum £300)
– deliberate but no concealment	70% of tax due (minimum £300)
– deliberate with concealment	100% of tax due (minimum £300)

Offence	Penalty
Late payment of tax	
− Paid > 1 month late	5% of tax due
− Paid > 6 months late	Additional 5%
− Paid > 12 months late	Additional 5%
	Applies to balancing payments only (not POAs).
Fraud or negligence on claiming reduced POAs	£
	POAs if claim not made X
	Less: POAs actually paid (X)
	___
	X
	___
Failure to keep and retain required records	Up to £3,000 per year of assessment

Note that 'tax' for an individual will include income tax, capital gains tax and NIC.

HMRC compliance checks

- HMRC has the right to enquire into the completeness and accuracy of any return.
- Must issue written notice before commencing a compliance check (enquiry).
  - within 12 months of the date the return is actually filed.
- On completion of a compliance check, HMRC must send the taxpayer a completion notice:
  - either stating no amendment required, or
  - amending the taxpayer's self assessment.
- Taxpayer has 30 days to appeal against HMRC's amendment.

Exam focus

Exam kit questions in this area:

Constructed response (section C) questions:

- Richard Feast
- Sophia Shape

Discovery assessments

- HMRC can raise a discovery assessment if they discover an inaccuracy in the return within:

	Time from end of tax year	For 2016/17
Basic time limit	Four years	5 April 2021
Careless error	Six years	5 April 2023
Deliberate error	Twenty years	5 April 2037

Appeals

Appeals to resolve disputes with HMRC

- Taxpayer can appeal against a decision made by HMRC
  - in writing
  - within 30 days of the disputed decision.
- They can proceed in one of two ways:
  - request a review by another HMRC officer, or
  - refer case to an independent Tax Tribunal.

Tax Tribunals

Two tiers (layers) of Tax Tribunal system:

- First-tier Tribunal, and
- Upper Tribunal.

The First-tier Tribunal deals with:

- Default paper cases:
  - simple appeals (e.g. against a fixed penalty)
  - usually no hearing provided both sides agree.
- Basic cases:
  - straightforward appeals
  - minimal exchange of paperwork
  - a short hearing.
- Standard cases:
  - more detailed consideration of issue
  - more formal hearing.

- Complex cases:
  - may be heard by the First-tier
  - however usually heard by Upper Tribunal.

The Upper Tribunal will deal with:

- Complex cases
  - requiring detailed specialist knowledge
  - a formal hearing.

Hearings are held in public and decisions are published.

A decision of the Upper Tribunal:

- may be appealed to the Court of Appeal
- but only on grounds of a point of law.

PAYE

- Under PAYE an employee's employment income tax liability is deducted from their remuneration and paid to HMRC by the employer.
- Each employee is given a code number to ensure that the tax collected at each pay date is the correct proportion of the tax due for the whole year.
- The code number is calculated from allowances and deductions.
- Allowances:
  - personal allowances
  - allowable interest paid
  - expenses deductible from earnings.

- Deductions:
  - benefits
  - any untaxed income on which the tax liability is discharged by set-off against allowances
  - any adjustment to cover tax underpaid in previous years (provided underpaid tax < £3,000).
- The code is 1/10th of net allowances rounded down to the nearest whole number.

Administration / forms

- Employers with less than 250 employees may make their monthly PAYE payments by cheque or electronically.
- Employers with 250 or more employees must pay electronically.
- PAYE/NIC payable to HMRC on 22nd of every month (electronic payment), or 19th if payments made by cheque.
- Employers with average monthly PAYE and NIC payments of £1,500:
  - can make quarterly payments
  - by 22nd of month following 5 July, 5 October, 5 January, 5 April (electronic payment).

Exam focus

As most employers now pay electronically, the pay day of 22nd of every month should be used in the examination.

Real time information (RTI)

- Employers must submit PAYE / NIC information to HMRC electronically when or before employees are paid each week or month.
- A year end summary = provided with the final RTI submission for the tax year.
- HMRC will charge penalties for late submissions of RTI:
  - no penalty is imposed for the first month that a late payment is made
  - a penalty of £100-£400 is applied for subsequent late payments. The amount depends on the number of employees
- An additional penalty of 5% of the PAYE/NIC due can be imposed once a payment is 3 month late.

Key forms

- P45 – when employee leaves.
- P60 – end of year summary
  – provided to employee by 31 May.
- P11D – summary of benefits
  – provided to employee by 6 July.

Exam focus

Constructed response (section C) questions:

- Long Ltd and Road Ltd

10

Capital gains tax: computation of gains and tax payable

In this chapter

- Chargeable gains.
- Tax payable.
- Chargeable individuals.
- CGT liability – individuals.
- Chargeable gain computation.
- Pro forma – CGT computation 2016/17.
- Capital losses.
- Transaction not at arm's length.
- Spouses and civil partners.
- Connected persons.
- Planning opportunities.

Chargeable gains could be tested in all three sections of the F6 examination.

It is therefore essential that you have a sound knowledge of the treatment of capital gains and that you understand the different treatment of gains by companies and individuals.

Chargeable gains

- A chargeable gain arises when:
  - a chargeable disposal is made
  - by a chargeable person
  - of a chargeable asset.

Tax payable

- Companies
  - pay corporation tax.
- Individuals
  - pay capital gains tax.

Chargeable gains

Chargeable persons
- individual
- company.

Chargeable assets
- all assets unless specifically exempt.

Chargeable disposals
- sale
- gift
- exchange
- loss/destruction of asset
- compensation for damage.

Exempt assets
Examples:
- motor cars
- non-wasting chattels bought & sold for <£6,000
- cash
- wasting chattels (e.g. horses, boats, caravan)
- qualifying corporate bonds (QCBs)
- individual's principal private residence
- assets held in ISAs.

Exempt disposals
- sale is a trading disposal
- transfers on death
- transfers to charity.

Exam focus

It is vital that you have learnt the key exempt assets, as these represent straightforward marks in the exam and could easily be the subject of an objective test question.

In written questions, you should state that the asset is exempt to score a mark, and not waste any time doing unnecessary calculations.

Chargeable individuals

Individuals are liable to CGT if they are resident in the UK.

Definition is the same as for income tax (see Chapter 1).

Chapter 10

CGT liability – individuals

- Individuals pay capital gains tax (CGT) on their taxable gains for a tax year.
- To calculate an individual's CGT liability:

  (1) Calculate the chargeable gains / allowable losses on the disposal of each chargeable asset separately.

  (2) Consider availability of any CGT reliefs (Chapter 12).

  (3) Calculate the net chargeable gains arising in the tax year
  = (chargeable gains less allowable losses).

  (4) Deduct capital losses brought forward.

  (5) Deduct the annual exempt amount (AEA) = taxable gains.

  (6) Calculate the CGT payable.

Chargeable gain computation

	Notes	£
Gross disposal proceeds	(1)	X
Less: Selling costs	(2)	(X)
Net disposal proceeds		X
Less: Allowable costs	(3)	(X)
Chargeable gain		X

Notes:

(1) Use market value where transaction not at arm's length.

(2) Include legal fees, advertising costs, etc.

(3) Include purchase price and purchase expenses (e.g. legal fees), and any capital enhancement expenditure.

Pro forma – CGT computation – 2016/17

	£
Net chargeable gains for the tax year (after specific reliefs)	X
Less: Capital losses b/f	(X)
	X
Less: AEA (2016/17)	(11,100)
Taxable gains	X
CGT (10% / 18% x gains in BRB)	X
(20% / 28% x gains above BRB)	X
	X

Due date	31 January 2018
	(i.e. 31 January after end of tax year)

CGT payable

- Taxable gains taxed as top slice of taxable income.
- Taxable gains in basic rate band (BRB) = taxed at 10% (18% if residential property)
- Taxable gains falling above BRB = taxed at 20% (28% if residential property)
- In addition, some gains may be taxed at 10% if entrepreneurs' relief is available (Chapter 12).

Exam focus

Exam kit questions in this area:

OT case (section B) questions:

- Albert and Charles

Constructed response (section C) questions

- Ginger and Nigel
- Mick Stone
- Ruby
- Pere Jones

Capital losses

Current year losses	Brought forward losses
Must be set off against current year chargeable gains.	Offset restricted to amount needed to reduce net chargeable gains down to the AEA amount (£11,100 for 2016/17).
Offset before brought forward losses.	
Cannot restrict the offset to preserve the AEA.	

Losses brought forward are only offset so far as to reduce the net chargeable gains down to the AEA.

Transaction not at arm's length

- Use market value instead of actual proceeds.
- Applies to:
  - gifts
  - disposals to connected persons (except married couple/civil partnership transfers).

Exam focus

For CGT purposes you need to know how to deal with transactions between spouses/ civil partners and also to be able to suggest simple tax planning opportunities.

Spouses and civil partners

For CGT purposes, married couple and civil partnership transfers are treated as follows:

- The connected persons rules are overridden.
- Spouse or civil partner transfers:
  - take place at nil gain/nil loss
  - regardless of any actual consideration which may have been received.
- The transferor is deemed to dispose of the asset at its acquisition cost
  - i.e. the spouse / civil partner takes over the asset at its original cost.

Exam focus

Exam kit questions in this area:

OT case (section B) questions

- Albert and Charles

Constructed response (section C) question

- Jerome

Connected persons

- At F6, an individual = connected with close relatives (i.e. parents, siblings, children).

- Consideration for disposal = Market value.

- Loss on disposal can only be offset against gains to same connected person.

Planning opportunities

- The ability to transfer assets between spouses/civil partners with no CGT consequences provides a number of opportunities:

  - ensure both spouses/civil partners use their AEAs each year

  - ensure gains are realised by the spouse/civil partner who has capital losses

  - ensure any taxable gains are realised by the spouse who has any basic rate band remaining.

Other CGT planning opportunities

- Delaying disposals until the following tax year can save tax:
  - if the AEA is available in the following year but not the current year.
  - if more BR band available in the following year than the current year.
- Delaying disposals until the following tax year will delay the payment of the associated CGT by 12 months.
- Selling assets piecemeal across different tax years to utilise more than one AEA will save tax.

11

Capital gains tax: special rules

In this chapter

- Part disposals.
- Chattels.
- Wasting assets.
- Insurance claims.
- Shares and securities.

Part disposals

Where only part of an asset is disposed of the cost is adjusted to reflect the cost of the part sold.

- Cost of part of asset disposed of:

$$\text{Cost} \times \frac{A}{A + B}$$ A = consideration
B = MV of the remainder

- Incidental costs which relate:
  - wholly to the part sold = fully deductible.
  - to the whole asset = apportioned as above (i.e. A/A + B).

Exam focus

Exam kit questions in this area:

OT case (section B) questions:

- Jorge Jung
- Acebook Ltd

Constructed response (section C) questions

- Mick Stone
- Jerome

Chattels

Tangible movable property
(e.g. painting, jewellery, racehorse, boat, caravan).

Wasting chattels:

*   expected life ≤ 50 years
    (e.g. racehorse, boat, caravan)
*   exempt from CGT unless plant & machinery on which capital allowances claimed.

Non-wasting chattels:

*   expected life > 50 years
    (e.g. antiques, paintings)
*   subject to £6,000 rule.

Exam kit questions in this area:

OT case (section B) questions:

*   Jorge Jung
*   Jerome

£6,000 Rule

Sale proceeds \ Cost	£6,000 or less	More than £6,000
£6,000 or less	Exempt	Allowable loss based on deemed proceeds of £6,000
More than £6,000	Normal gain computation but gain cannot exceed: 5/3 x (Gross SP – £6,000)	Normal gain computation

Wasting assets

Wasting assets (life ≤ 50 years)

Chattels
(i.e. tangible and movable)

Not Chattels
(e.g. copyright royalties)

Not eligible for capital allowances (e.g. greyhound)

Eligible for capital allowances (e.g. plant and machinery used in a trade)

Normal gain computation but Allowable cost is calculated as:

$$\text{Cost} \times \frac{\text{Remaining life at disposal}}{\text{Estimated useful life}}$$

Exempt

- Normal gains computation subject to £6,000 chattels rule unless a loss.
- No allowable capital loss arises as capital allowances already given relief for loss in CAs computation (i.e. fall in value of asset).

Insurance claims

Different treatment depending on whether:

- Asset lost or destroyed.
- Asset damaged.

Assets lost or destroyed

```
                    ┌─────────────────────────┐
                    │   Asset lost or destroyed │
                    │     – deemed disposal     │
                    └─────────────────────────┘
```

┌──────────────────┐   ┌──────────────────┐
│ No insurance   │   │   Insurance   │
│ proceeds   │   │   proceeds received │
└──────────────────┘   └──────────────────┘

┌──────────────┐   ┌──────────────┐   ┌──────────────┐   ┌──────────────────────────┐
│ Normal   │   │   │   │ Reinvested   │   │ Partially re-invested   │
│ computation: │   │ Not   │   │ within 12 months: │ │ within 12 months: │
│ Capital loss │   │ reinvested: │   │ Elect for no gain/ │ │ – immediate gain =   │
│   │   │ Normal   │   │ no loss   │   │   proceeds not re-invested │
│   │   │ computation │   │   │   │ – Rollover remaining gain. │
└──────────────┘   └──────────────┘   └──────────────┘   └──────────────────────────┘

Exam focus

Exam kit questions in this area:

OT case (section B) questions:

- Acebook Ltd

Asset damaged

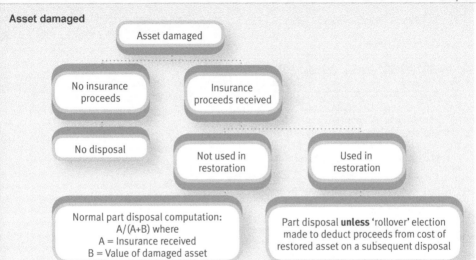

Asset damaged

No insurance proceeds

Insurance proceeds received

No disposal

Not used in restoration

Used in restoration

Normal part disposal computation:
A/(A+B) where
A = Insurance received
B = Value of damaged asset

Part disposal **unless** 'rollover' election made to deduct proceeds from cost of restored asset on a subsequent disposal

Exam focus

Exam kit questions in this area:

OT case (section B) questions:

- Acebook Ltd

Shares and securities

Valuation rules

Transaction:	Consideration:
Sale	Sale proceeds
Gift	Market value
Transfer to a connected person	Market value

Market value of quoted shares:

- Mid price (i.e. average) of quoted price in SE Daily Official List on disposal date.

Matching rules

Apply where an individual has made more than one purchase of shares of the same class in the same company.

Disposals matched with:

(1) Acquisitions on same day.

(2) Acquisitions in the next 30 days.

(3) The share pool (shares acquired before the date of disposal are pooled together)

Exam focus

Exam kit questions in this area:

OT case (section B) questions:

- Albert and Charles
- Acebook Ltd

Constructed response (section C) questions

- Ginger and Nigel
- Mick Stone
- Ruby
- Luna Ltd

Disposal of shares by individuals

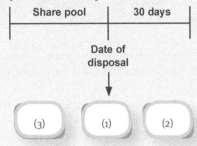

Share pool	30 days

Date of disposal

Step 1 Determine the sale proceeds per share.

Step 2 Identify the date the shares are purchased and using the matching rules allocate the disposal to the time periods above.

Step 3 Compute the gains and losses on disposals of shares from each matching rule.

The share pool

- The share pool contains shares in the same company, of the same class, purchased before the date of a disposal.
- It contains the amalgamated cost of shares acquired.
- The cost of shares disposed of is calculated as a proportion of the number of shares removed from the pool.
- If an individual disposes of shares:
  - in his personal trading company, and
  - is also an employee of that company

  entrepreneurs' relief (ER) is available (see Chapter 12).

Bonus issues

Definition

Distribution of free shares to shareholders based on their existing shareholding.

For CGT purposes bonus issues are treated as follows:

- The bonus shares are not treated as a separate holding of shares.
- The shares are treated as acquired on the same day as the original shares to which they relate.
- Therefore, the number of bonus shares are included in the share pool but at nil cost.

Rights issues

Definition

Offer of new shares to existing shareholders in proportion to their existing shareholding, usually at a price below the market price.

For CGT purposes rights issues are treated as follows:

- The rights shares are not treated as a separate holding of shares.
- The shares are treated as acquired on the same day as the original shares to which they relate.
- Therefore, the number of rights shares are included in the share pool, and the cost in the cost column in the same way as a normal purchase.

Reorganisations/takeovers

Reorganisation:
exchange of existing shares for shares of another class in the same company.

Takeover:
when a company acquires shares in another company either in exchange for shares in itself, cash or a mixture of both.

For CGT purposes reorganisations and takeovers are automatically treated as shown in the following diagram.

Exam kit questions in this area:

Constructed response (section C) questions:

- Luna Ltd

```
                    ┌──────────────────┐
                    │  Consideration   │
                    └──────────────────┘
              ┌────────────┴────────────┐
    ┌──────────────────┐      ┌──────────────────┐
    │  Share for share │      │  Cash and        │
    │                  │      │  shares          │
    └──────────────────┘      └──────────────────┘
```

Share for share
- No CGT disposal at time of takeover/reorganisation
- Cost of the original shares becomes the cost of the new shares

Cash and shares
- Part disposal of the original shares
- A = Cash received
- B = Market value of new shares
- Gain arises on the cash element of the consideration

chapter 12

Capital gains tax: reliefs for individuals

In this chapter

- Overview of reliefs.
- Entrepreneurs' relief (ER).
- Investors' relief (IR).
- Principal private residence relief (PPR).
- Rollover relief (ROR).
- Gift relief (GR).

Overview of reliefs

- After computing gains on disposals of individual assets consider the availability of reliefs.
- Some reliefs completely exempt a gain from CGT, or reduce the tax payable permanently, others only defer the gain to a later period.

Types of relief	
Permanent reliefs	**Deferral reliefs**
Entrepreneurs' relief	Rollover relief
Investors' relief	Gift relief
PPR relief	
Letting relief	

Key Point

- The reliefs are normally applied to the capital gains before deducting capital losses, except entrepreneurs' relief and investors' relief (see later).

Entrepreneurs' relief (ER)

- Only available to individuals.

- First £10 million of gains on 'qualifying business disposals' are taxed at 10%, regardless of the taxpayer's income.

- Any gains above the £10 million limit = taxed in full at 10%/20%.

- Gains qualifying for ER are set against any remaining BR band before non-qualifying gains.

- The 10% CGT rate is calculated **after** the deduction of:

  - allowable losses, and

  - the AEA.

- Can choose to set losses and AEA against non-qualifying gains first to maximise relief.

  Exception:

  any losses on assets forming part of the disposal of the business.

- Keep gains which qualify for ER separate from those which do not qualify.

- For 2016/17 disposals, the relief must be claimed by 31 January 2019.

- £10 million = a lifetime limit (partly used up each time a claim is made).

Qualifying business disposals

The disposal of:

- the whole or part of an individual's trading business (i.e. sole trader or partner)
- assets of the individual's or partnership's trading business that has **now ceased**
- shares **provided**:
  - shares = in the individual's 'personal trading company', and
  - the individual = an employee of the company (part time or full time).

An individual's 'personal trading company' = where the individual:

- owns at least 5% of the ordinary shares
- which carry at least 5% of the voting rights.

Note that:

- "Part of a business"
  = a "substantial part" which is "capable independent operation".
- Disposal of assets (i.e. not shares): Relief = not available on investment assets.
- No restriction to relief if company holds non-trading assets.
- No minimum working hours to satisfy employee condition.

Key Point

The isolated disposal of an **individual business asset** used for the purposes of a continuing trade does **not** qualify.

Qualifying ownership period

- Disposal of:
  - Individual's trading business = business owned for 12 months
  - Shares = individual's personal trading company and employee for 12 months
- Where a qualifying business is not disposed of but simply ceases:
  - relief will be available on gains on assets in use in the business at the time it ceased
  - where the assets are disposed of within 3 years of the date of cessation, and
  - the business has been owned for 12 months prior to cessation.

Applying the relief

(1) Calculate the gains and losses on qualifying and non-qualifying assets separately.

(2) Net off losses relating to the qualifying business disposals against qualifying gains.

(3) Offset all other losses and the AEA against non-qualifying gains.

(4) If necessary, deduct any remaining losses or AEA from the qualifying gains.

(5) Tax the gains as follows:
  - qualifying net chargeable gains at 10%.
  - non-qualifying net chargeable gains as normal at 10% or 20% (remember that qualifying gains utilise the BR band before non-qualifying gains). The rates increase to 18% or 28% where residential property is disposed of.

Exam focus

Exam kit questions in this area:

Constructed response (section C) question:

- Michael and Sean
- Ginger and Nigel
- Mick Stone
- Ruby

Interaction of reliefs

- Other specific reliefs (if available) reduce chargeable gains before ER is considered.
- If also eligible for ER the remaining gain is taxable at 10%.

Investors' relief (IR)

ER is only available if:

- the shares are in the individual's personal company (they hold 5%), and

- they are an officer or employee of the company.

From 6 April 2016, investors' relief has been introduced which extends the benefits of ER to certain investors who would not meet the conditions for ER.

IR applies to the disposal of:

- unlisted ordinary shares in a trading company (including AIM shares)

- subscribed for (i.e. newly issued shares) on/after 17 March 2016

- which have been held for a minimum period of 3 years starting on 6 April 2016

- by an individual that is not an employee of the company.

- IR is subject to a separate lifetime limit of £10 million of qualifying gains.

- Claims for IR cannot be made before the tax year 2019/20 due to the 3 year minimum holding period.

- Therefore in the F6 examination you must not apply IR to gains arising before the tax year 2019/20.

Principal private residence relief (PPR)

PPR

Occupied throughout

Gain exempt

Occupied for part of period of ownership

- Calculate gain
- PPR relief:

  Gain x $\dfrac{\text{Periods of occupation}}{\text{Period of ownership}}$

Let

- Deduct PPR relief
- Then give letting relief:

  Lowest of:

  (i) £40,000

  (ii) PPR relief

  (iii) Gain re-letting perio

PPR – Periods of occupation

- Actual occupation.
- Deemed occupation.

Exam focus

You may be presented with an individual's personal circumstances and be required to determine the period of ownership of a property which will qualify for PPR.

You should provide brief explanatory notes for periods of deemed occupation, as these will earn marks.

Exam focus

Exam kit questions in this area:

Constructed response (section C) question:

- Albert and Charles

Deemed occupation

Conditional	Unconditional
• Up to 3 years – any reason • Any period – employed abroad • Up to 4 years – working elsewhere in the UK (employed or self-employed) • Must be actual occupation before and after • Condition relaxed if reoccupation prevented by terms of employment	• Last 18 months of ownership

Rollover relief (ROR)

- Relief for the replacement of qualifying business assets (QBAs).
- The gain arising on the disposal of a QBA is deferred where the net sale proceeds are reinvested in a replacement QBA within a qualifying period.
- Available to:
  - individual sole traders, partnerships and companies.

Key Point

ROR is the only relief available to companies.

Exam focus

Exam kit questions in this area:

Constructed response (section C) question:

- Mick Stone

Conditions

Disposal of and reinvestment

in Qualifying asset:	within Qualifying time period:
· Land & buildings · Fixed plant & machinery · Goodwill (unincorporated businesses only) Must be used in the trade	From 12 months before to 36 months after the sale

Effect of relief

Where net sale proceeds are reinvested:

- The full gain on the old asset is 'rolled over' against the capital gains cost of the new asset.
- No tax payable when the old asset sold.
- Gain deferred until the new asset sold.

Deferred gain is:

- deducted from the base cost of the replacement asset, and
- deferred until the subsequent disposal of the replacement asset.

Claim for relief

- Within 4 years from the later of the end of the tax year of:
  - sale, and
  - replacement.
- For a 2016/17 disposal and replacement; by 5 April 2021.

Partial reinvestment of proceeds

Where net sales proceeds are **not** all reinvested:

- The gain that can be rolled over (i.e. deferred) is restricted (i.e. not all of the gain can be deferred).
- A chargeable gain arises = **lower** of:
  - the proceeds not reinvested
  - the chargeable gain.
- Taxable on the disposal of the original asset.
- The remaining gain can be deferred.

Reinvestment in depreciating assets

Definition

Depreciating asset (DA)

- life of $\leqslant$ 60 years.

Common examples in the F6 examination:

- Fixed P&M
- Leasehold property of $\leqslant$ 60 years.

Method of relief

- Conditions and calculation of amount of relief = same as for ROR.
- Method of deferral = different.
- Gain not deducted from base cost of new asset.
- Gain is 'frozen' (i.e. deferred) and crystallises on the earliest of:
    - sale of DA
    - date DA ceases to be used in trade
    - 10 years from acquisition of DA.
- When deferred gain crystallises:
    - taxed at appropriate rate of CGT at that time (not at the time of deferral)

- Can defer a gain using a depreciating asset (for up to 10 years) and later acquire a non-depreciating asset and claim to rollover the deferred gain instead (i.e. defer indefinitely until the replacement non-depreciating asset is sold).
  - provided the deferred gain has not previously become chargeable.

ROR may be examined in a question dealing with either an individual or a company.

Remember that ROR is the only relief available to companies. It is therefore more often tested in a corporate situation.

Gift relief (GR)

Key Point

The gain arising on a gift is calculated using the market value of the asset.

GR must then be considered.

Exam focus

Exam kit questions in this area:

OT case (section B) questions:

- Jorge Jung

Constructed response (section C) questions:

- Ginger and Nigel
- Jerome

Conditions

- GR applies to gifts:
  - by individuals
  - of business assets.
- Business assets:
  - Assets used in a trade by the donor or his personal trading company (i.e. donor holds ≥ 5% of shares).
  - Shares in:
    - an unquoted trading company
    - the donor's personal trading company.

    Note: no requirement to work for company.
- For a gift in 2016/17, a joint election is required:
  - signed by both the donor and donee
  - by 5 April 2021 (i.e. within 4 years from the end of the tax year in which the gift was made).

Effect of relief

- No chargeable gain arises on donor at time of gift.
- Higher gain arises on donee later.
- The gain is deferred against the donee's base cost of the asset.
- The donee in effect takes over the donor's gain which will be taxed when the donee disposes of the asset.

The deferred gain is:

- deducted from the base cost of the donee, and
- deferred until the subsequent disposal of the asset by the donee.

When the deferred gain crystallises:

- taxed at appropriate rate of CGT at that time (not at the time of deferral).

Sale at undervaluation

Where the asset is sold, but for less than MV, the 'actual consideration' received is ignored:

- The gain is still calculated using MV.

If the actual consideration > donor's cost:

- the excess is immediately chargeable
- the remaining gain can be deferred.

The chargeable gain arising now will be:

- taxed on the donor at either 0%, 10% or 20%
- depending on the availability of the AEA, ER or the level of taxable income.

If the actual consideration ≤ donor's cost:

- full gift relief available
- all chargeable gain deferred.

The deferred gain is taxed on the donee later at the appropriate rate when they dispose of the asset.

Non-business use

- The GR is restricted where there is non-business use of the asset.
- For shares in a personal trading company:
  - the gain eligible for relief is:

    $$\text{Gain} \times \frac{\text{MV of company's CBA}}{\text{MV of company's CA}}$$

    Where
    CBA = chargeable business assets
    CA = chargeable assets
  - GR is available regardless of whether the individual works for the company.
  - any chargeable gain arising now will be taxed on the donor at 0%, 10% or 20% depending on the availability of the AEA, ER or the level of taxable income.
  - The deferred gain is taxed on the donee later at the appropriate rate when they dispose of the shares.

- If the donor holds less than 5% of the shares (i.e. it is not their personal trading company):
  - for unquoted shares
    - full relief is available (the restriction does not apply)
  - for quoted shares
    - GR is not available.

13

Inheritance tax

In this chapter

- Charge to inheritance tax.
- Lifetime gifts.
- IHT computations.
- Diminution in value.
- Due dates of payment.
- Exemptions.
- Pro forma – Death estate.
- Married couples and civil partners.
- Lifetime giving.
- Skipping a generation.

Inheritance tax could be tested in all three sections of the examination.

Charge to inheritance tax (IHT)

- Occasions of charge:
    - Lifetime gifts.
    - Death estate.
- Charged on:
    - a chargeable transfer (see later)
    - of chargeable property
    - by a chargeable person.
- Chargeable property:
    - all capital assets / wealth
    - no exempt assets for IHT.
- Chargeable person:
    - individuals.
- Gratuitous intent:
    - transfer must be a gift
    - intention to give asset away
    - not a poor business deal.

Lifetime gifts

- Two types:
  - Potentially Exempt Transfers (PETs)
  - Chargeable Lifetime Transfers (CLTs).

	PETs	CLTs	
Definition	Gift by individual to another individual	Gift which is not: • Exempt; or • a PET For F6 = gift into a trust	
Chargeable	Only if donor dies within 7 years of gift	At date of gift	Additional IHT if donor dies within 7 years of gift
Tax rates	Death rates	Lifetime rates	Death rates
Tax paid by	Donee	Donee, or Donor (if so; gross up gift for tax paid)	Donee

IHT computations

An IHT charge can arise in 3 different situations. The computation in each situation is different and must be studied carefully.

(1) Lifetime transfers – IHT on CLTs.

(2) Death – additional IHT on PETs and CLTs.

(3) Death estate.

In each situation:

- Stage 1: Compute the chargeable transfer.
- Stage 2: Compute the taxable amount.
- Stage 3: Compute the tax.

Stage 1: The chargeable transfer

The first stage of the computation for each situation is always the same; compute the chargeable transfer:

	£	
Transfer of value:		
Value before	X	Diminution in
Value after	(X)	value principle
	——	
	X	
Deduct:		
Exemptions	(X)	See below
Chargeable transfer	A	

Order of exemptions:

(1) Small gifts, inter spouse and civil partner gifts.

(2) Marriage exemption.

(3) AE – current year, then b/fwd.

Diminution in value

Gifts

*   IHT uses the 'diminution in value' principle to calculate the 'transfer of value' (i.e. value by which the donor's estate has been reduced as a result of the gift).

	£
Value of estate before transfer	X
Value of estate after transfer	(X)
Transfer of value	X

*   In most cases the transfer of value = value of asset gifted.

*   In some cases the fall in value of the estate > value of the asset gifted (e.g. gift of unquoted shares).

 Key Point

It is important to appreciate the difference here between CGT and IHT.

*   For CGT purposes:
    *   a gift is always valued at the market value of the asset gifted, at the time of the gift.

Stage 2: Calculating the taxable amount

Stage 2 is also the same for each situation. However, the calculation of the available nil rate band (NRB) differs.

	£
Chargeable transfer	A
Less:	
Available NRB	(X)
Taxable amount	X

Nil rate bands (NRB)

- For lifetime gifts – lifetime tax:
  - Use NRB in tax year of gift.
- For lifetime gifts – death tax:
  - Use NRB in tax year of death.
- For death estate:
  - Use NRB in tax year of death.
- The NRBs will be provided in the examination where needed.

Exam focus

Exam kit questions in this area:

OT case (section B) questions:

- Ning Gao
- Afiya

Constructed response (section C) questions

- Rosie and Tom
- Pere Jones
- Kendra Older
- Marcus

Stage 3: Calculating the tax

1 – Lifetime tax on CLT (example – gift in 2008/09)

	£	£
Chargeable transfer (A)		222,000
Less:		
NRB at gift (2008/09)	312,000	
Less: CLTs in 7 years prior to gift (say)	(170,000)	
NRB available		(142,000)
Taxable amount		80,000
IHT payable:		
(i) at 20% if donee pays tax		16,000
(ii) at 25% if donor pays tax		20,000

If donor pays tax:
Add IHT to value of chargeable transfer (A) to calculate gross chargeable amount (B) (£222,000 + £20,000) = £242,000.

Key Point

Note that the donor is primarily responsible for the lifetime tax due.

2 – Additional tax on lifetime transfers as a result of donor's death (example – death in 2016/17)

Perform the following calculation for:

- each gift (CLTs and PETs) in the 7 years prior to death
- in chronological order.

Gift 1 – CLT or PET

	£	£
Gross chargeable transfer (A or B)		365,000
Less:		
NRB at death	325,000	
Less: CLTs and chargeable PETs in 7 years prior to gift 1 (say)	(140,000)	
NRB available		(185,000)
Taxable amount		180,000

	£
IHT payable at 40%	72,000
Less: Taper relief (40%)(say)	(28,800)
Chargeable (60%)	43,200
Less: Lifetime tax paid (say)	(10,000)
IHT payable	33,200

Then perform the same calculation for gift 2 etc.

Taper relief

Years before death	% reduction
Over 3 but less than 4 years	20%
Over 4 but less than 5 years	40%
Over 5 but less than 6 years	60%
Over 6 but less than 7 years	80%

Lifetime tax deduction

- Cannot create a repayment of IHT.

3 – IHT on death estate

Death estate computation:

	£	£
Value of Estate		925,000
Less:		
NRB at death	325,000	
Less: CLTs and chargeable PETs in 7 years prior to death (say)	(180,000)	
NRB available		(145,000)
Taxable amount		780,000
IHT payable at 40%		312,000

Exam focus

Exam kit questions in this area:

OT case (section B) questions:

- Ning Gao
- Afiya

Constructed response (section C) questions:

- Pere Jones
- Kendra Older
- James

Due dates of payment

1   Lifetime IHT

Gift:	Due date:
6 April – 30 Sept	30 April in next year
1 Oct – 5 April	6 months after end of month of gift

2   Additional IHT on lifetime gifts due to death

Due date – 6 months from end of month of death.

Note: always paid by donee.

3   IHT on death estate

Due date – 6 months from end of month of death.

However, tax is required to be paid with delivery of accounts to HMRC, which may be earlier than due date.

Exemptions

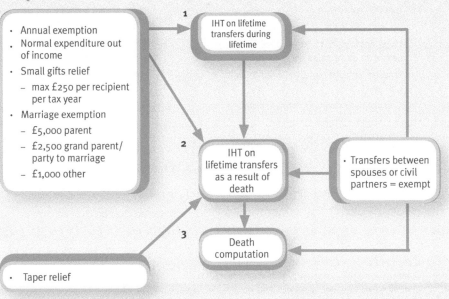

- Annual exemption
- Normal expenditure out of income
- Small gifts relief
  - max £250 per recipient per tax year
- Marriage exemption
  - £5,000 parent
  - £2,500 grand parent/ party to marriage
  - £1,000 other

1 → IHT on lifetime transfers during lifetime

2 → IHT on lifetime transfers as a result of death

3 → Death computation

- Transfers between spouses or civil partners = exempt

- Taper relief

Annual exemption

- £3,000 per annum.
- Applied to gifts in chronological order.
- Used against PET – even if PET never becomes chargeable.
- Unused amount can be carried forward one year.
- Current year exemption used in priority to brought forward.
- Applied after all other reliefs and exemptions have been applied.

Normal expenditure out of income

- Gift is exempt if made as part of normal expenditure out of income (not capital).
- Must not effect donor's standard of living
- Must be habitual.
- Level will depend on income of donor.

Exam focus

Exam kit questions in this area:

OT case (section B) questions:

- Afiya

Constructed response (section C) questions

- Pere Jones
- Marcus

Exam focus

Exemptions are likely to feature in an IHT computation – it is important that you can identify when they are available and how they are applied.

Pro forma – Death estate

	Notes	£
Freehold property		x
Less: Mortgage	(a)	(x)
		x
Motor car		x
Life insurance proceeds	(b)	x
Cash and bank accounts (including ISAs)		x
All other assets owned by deceased		x
Debts due to deceased		x
		x
Less: Outstanding debts	(c)	(x)
Funeral expenses		(x)
		x
Less: Exempt legacies	(d)	(x)
Chargeable estate		**x**
Inheritance tax payable		x

Paid by: Executors = personal representatives

Tax on death estate is usually suffered by:

- the residual legatee (i.e. recipient of 'the rest' of the death estate)
- not those receiving specific gifts.

Notes

(a) Repayment and interest-only mortgages and accrued interest. Do not deduct an endowment mortgage.

(b) Use the insurance policy proceeds, not the market value at the date of death.

(c) Outstanding debts payable by the deceased and incurred for valuable consideration (e.g. outstanding bills, other taxes due: IT, CGT, VAT). Not gambling debts or a promise to pay a friend.

(d) Exempt legacies = legacies to spouse or civil partner.

Key Point

All assets are chargeable
(i.e. no exempt assets for IHT at F6).

Assets that are exempt from CGT
(e.g. motor cars, gilts, ISAs, PPR, etc.)
are not exempt from IHT.

Exam focus

Exam kit questions in this area:

OT case (section B) questions:

- Ning Gao

Constructed response (section C) questions:

- Kendra Older

Married couples and civil partners

Transfer of unused NRB

- If the NRB has not been utilised at the time of a person's death, the proportion of the unused NRB can be transferred to their spouse or civil partner.

- At their death, the surviving spouse or civil partner will have the benefit of:

  - their own NRB, **and**

  - any unused percentage of their spouse's or civil partner's NRB.

- The unused percentage is applied to the NRB at the time of the surviving spouse or civil partner's death

  - **not** at the date of the first death.

- The executors of the surviving spouse or civil partner must claim the transferred NRB by the submission of the IHT return by the later of:

  - 2 years of the second death, or

  - 3 months of the executors starting to act.

- As a result, each spouse or civil partner can leave the whole of their estate to the surviving spouse or civil partner with no adverse IHT consequences.

Exam focus

Exam kit questions in this area:

OT case (section B) questions:

- Ning Gao

Lifetime giving

Advantage of lifetime gifts	Disadvantages of lifetime gifts

• Reduces IHT payable on death as assets gifted during lifetime are removed from the chargeable estate.
 	
 • IHT on lifetime gifts likely to be less than IHT in death estate because:
   – IHT = Nil (for a PET), and 20% (for a CLT) if the donor lives for at least 7 years
   – the value of the gift is frozen at the date of the gift, therefore by gifting an appreciating asset during lifetime, if IHT becomes chargeable, it is based on a lower amount
   – lifetime exemptions such AE, ME, small gifts and normal gifts out of income are available
   – taper relief is available if the donor lives for at least 3 years.
	• Loss of income and use of the capital asset if given away.
	
	 • IHT is not the only tax that needs to be considered re lifetime gifts:
	   – the impact of CGT is also an important consideration.

Skipping a generation

- Gifting to grandchildren rather than children avoids a further IHT charge when the children die.

- Such planning requires children to be independently wealthy, so that they have no need for the inheritance.

Exam focus

Exam kit questions in this area:

Constructed response (section C) questions:

- James

14

Outline of corporation tax

In this chapter

- Principles of corporation tax.
- Chargeable accounting periods.
- Pro forma – corporation tax.
- Trading income.
- Property income.
- Interest.
- Qualifying charitable donations.
- Long period of account.

Exam focus

Corporation tax is an important topic area of the syllabus.

It will be the focus of a 15 mark question in section C.

It is also very likely to be tested in both sections A and B.

Principles of corporation tax

Companies **resident** in the UK pay corporation tax on their **worldwide** profits (including chargeable gains but excluding dividends).

Definition

A company is resident in the UK if it is:

- incorporated in the UK, or
- it is an overseas company and its central management and control is exercised in the UK.

Companies pay corporation tax on their taxable total profits (TTP) for a chargeable accounting period (CAP).

Chargeable accounting periods (CAPs)

- A CAP is usually the company's period of account (i.e. the period for which the company prepares its accounts).

- A CAP cannot exceed 12 months.

- If a period of account exceeds 12 months, the period is split into 2 CAP's (see later).

A CAP can be any length up to 12 months but can never exceed 12 months.

Pro forma – corporation tax

Corporation tax computation for the chargeable accounting period of…months ended…

	Notes	£
Trading profit	(1)	X
Less: Loss relief b/f		(X)
		X
Property income		X
Interest income	(2)	X
Chargeable gains	(3)	X
Total profits		X
Less: Loss relief – CY, C/B		(X)
Less: QCD relief	(4)	(X)
		X
Less: Group relief		(X)
Taxable total profits (TTP)		X
Corporation tax: TTP x 20% (5)		X

It is essential to learn and use this pro forma

Notes

(1) Tax adjusted trading profit less capital allowances.

(2) Net interest income on non-trade loan relationships.

(3) Chargeable gains net of current year and brought forward capital losses.

(4) Qualifying charitable donations (QCDs) = all charitable donations by a company (except those allowed as a trading expense) (see later).

(5) The rate of corporation tax is fixed for each financial year. The rate for FY2016 is 20%.

Key Point

Dividends received from UK companies are exempt, and therefore are:

- not included in TTP, and
- not subject to corporation tax.

Exam focus

When calculating the TTP:

(i) Start your answer by laying out the CT pro forma, listing all income types and deducting QCDs.

(ii) Prepare separate workings for each element of the computation. Insert the relevant figures in the pro forma and cross-reference the figures clearly.

Exam focus

Exam kit questions in this area:

Constructed response (section C) questions:

- Heavy Ltd
- Softapp Ltd
- E-commerce plc
- Lucky Ltd
- Clueless Ltd
- Long Ltd and Road Ltd

Trading income

A company's trading profit is adjusted for tax purposes.

Adjustment to profits and capital allowances for companies

Computed in the same way as for individuals (Chapters 3 and 4) except for:

- no private use adjustments
- interest payable/receivable
  - loan relationship rules apply
- capital allowances
  - no private use assets
  - where period of account > 12 months, separate capital allowance computations required for each CAP.

Property income

The rules for calculating property income are the same as for individuals (Chapter 1) except as follows:

- company is assessed on the profit arising in the CAP (not the tax year)
- interest payable on a loan to acquire investment property is deducted from interest income (not property income as for an individual)
- no rent-a-room relief
- treatment of property losses (see below)

Property losses

- Property income and losses on different properties are pooled.
- If there is a net loss in one CAP:
  - set first against total profits (before QCDs) of the same CAP
  - any excess loss is carried forward to be offset against total profits before QCDs) in the future.

Exam focus

Exam kit questions in this area:

Constructed response (section C) questions:

- Softapp Ltd
- E-commerce plc

Interest

Interest income

- Assessed according to the loan relationship rules.
- In the F6 examination all interest is received gross by a company.
- All interest receivable and payable on loans used for non-trading purposes is taxed as interest income.
- Incidental costs of raising loan finance such as arrangement fees and loans written off are also dealt with under these rules.

- In the exam – assume that all interest receivable is for non-trade purposes (e.g. interest receivable on bank/building society accounts).
- Deduct interest receivable in adjustment to profits computation.
- Include in CT computation as interest income.
- Tax on the accruals basis.

Exam focus

Exam kit questions in this area:

Constructed response (section C) questions:

- Softapp Ltd
- E-commerce plc
- Lucky Ltd
- Clueless Ltd
- Long Ltd and Road Ltd

Interest payable

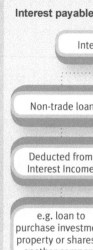

- Interest paid is deductible on the accruals basis.

Qualifying charitable donations (QCDs)

- Relief is available for all charitable donations made by a company:
  - Small donations to local charities = allowable trading expense
  - other charitable donations = allowable deductions from total profits, known as QCD relief.
- The amount paid in the CAP is deducted from total profits.
- All charitable donations by companies = paid gross.
- If QCD relief exceeds total profits:
  - no relief available for the excess (unless part of a group) (see Chapter 17).

Long period of account

Accounting period > 12 months must be split into two CAPs:

- First 12 months
- Remainder.

For each CAP, HMRC require:

- a separate CT comp, and
- a separate CT return.

Note there will be:

- Two separate pay days (i.e. 9 months after end of CAP)
- But only one file date for the returns (i.e. 12 months after end of long period of account).

Splitting the profits:

Tax adjusted trading profit before CAs	Time-apportion
Capital allowances	Separate computations (where the CAP is less than 12 months, the WDA/AIA is reduced accordingly, but not FYA)
Interest/Property/Other income	Calculate accrued amount for each period separately (Note)
Chargeable gains	According to date of disposal
Qualifying charitable donations	According to date paid

Note: if information to apply the strict accruals basis is not available; time apportion.

15

Chargeable gains for companies

In this chapter

- Introduction.
- Capital losses.
- Chargeable gain computation.
- Indexation allowance.
- Enhancement expenditure.
- Shares and securities.
- Rollover relief.
- Summary of key differences.

Introduction

- Companies pay corporation tax on net chargeable gains arising in a CAP.

- To calculate net chargeable gains:

    Step 1: Calculate the chargeable gains/losses arising on each asset disposed of in a CAP

    Step 2: Aggregate the gains/losses:

	£
Gain (transaction 1)	X
Gain (transaction 2)	X
Loss (transaction 3)	(X)
Net gains in period	X
Less: Capital losses b/f	(X)
Net chargeable gains	A

    Step 3: Include the net chargeable gains (A) in the company's TTP.

Capital losses

- Capital losses are set off against gains arising in the same CAP.

- Unutilised losses are carried forward and set against chargeable gains of future CAPs.

- Capital losses cannot be set off against any other income of the company.

- See Chapter 16 for further details.

Chargeable gain computation

The individual gains/losses are calculated in the same way as for individuals (i.e. disposal proceeds less allowable expenditure) however:

- the only relief available to companies is rollover relief (ROR)
- IA is available
- different matching rules apply for shares and securities.

Key Point

A company's capital gains and losses are calculated according to the principles of CGT but it pays corporation tax and not CGT on its chargeable gains.

Indexation allowance (IA)

- IA is available up to the date of disposal.
- IA is based on the retail price index (RPI):

  IA = Cost x Indexation factor

  Formula: Indexation factor

  $$\frac{\text{RPI month of disposal} - \text{RPI month of acquisition}}{\text{RPI month of acquisition}}$$

- Indexation factor is rounded to three decimal places (exception = shares in share pool).
- IA cannot increase or create a loss.
- If there is a fall in the RPI between acquisition and disposal: IA = £Nil.

Enhancement expenditure

- Additional capital expenditure is an allowable cost (e.g. improvements such as building extensions).

- IA is given on the enhancement expenditure from the date that expenditure was incurred.

- Separate IA calculations will be required for the original cost and the enhancement expenditure.

Shares and securities

Valuation rules

The valuation rules for shares are the same as for individuals (Chapter 11).

Matching rules

For companies, shares of the same type are matched as follows:

(1) Same day acquisitions.

(2) Shares acquired in the previous 9 days (FIFO basis).

(3) Acquisitions in share pool.

Calculation of gains

- No IA is given on same day acquisitions and purchases in the previous 9 days.

- IA is available on the share pool shares (see below).

The share pool

Use the following pro forma for the share pool for companies:

	Number	Cost	Indexed cost
		£	£
Purchase	X	X	X
Index to next event			X
Purchase	X	X	X
	X	X	X
Index to next event			X
	X	X	X
Sale	(X)	(X)^{W1}	(X)^{W2}
Pool c/f	X	X	X

W1

$$\frac{\text{Number of shares sold}}{\text{Number of shares in pool}} \times \text{Cost to date}$$

W2

$$\frac{\text{Number of shares sold}}{\text{Number of shares in pool}} \times \text{Indexed cost to date}$$

Notes

- Indexation is calculated every time an operative event occurs (e.g. sale, purchase, rights issue).
- Do not index up before a bonus issue.
- Indexation is not rounded to three decimal places in the share pool.

Bonus and rights issues

- A bonus issue is not an operative event in the share pool:
  - just add number of shares into pool, nil cost.
- A rights issue is an operative event:
  - index up to the date of the rights issue
  - add number of shares and then the cost of shares to both the cost and indexed cost in the pool.

Reorganisations and takeovers

The rules are the same as for individuals (Chapter 11), except:

- Must take account of IA.
- IA should be calculated up to date of takeover, then again when the new shares are sold.
- Acceptable shortcut = index from acquisition to disposal date of shares.

Exam focus

Exam kit questions in this area:

OT case (section B) questions:

- Acebook Ltd

Constructed response (section C) questions:

- Luna Ltd

Rollover relief (ROR)

The rules for ROR are the same for companies as they are for individuals except:

- The gain deferred is the 'indexed gain'.
- Goodwill is not a qualifying asset for a company.
- The key categories of qualifying business assets (QBA) are:
  - land and buildings
  - fixed plant and machinery.
- In particular, note that a freehold or leasehold interest in land and buildings is a QBA, but if the leasehold is for < 60 years on acquisition the gain can only be deferred for a maximum of 10 years.
- The claim deadline for companies is within four years of the later of the end of the accounting period in which the asset is:
  - sold, and
  - replaced.

Exam focus

ROR is the only major capital gains relief available to companies. It is therefore more likely to be tested in the examination in a corporate based question.

Summary of key differences

	Company	Individual
Tax paid	Corporation tax	Capital gains tax
AEA	Not available	2016/17 = £11,100
Indexation allowance	Available for full period of ownership	Not available
Capital losses b/f	Offset in full	Offset restricted so net gains = AEA
Shares and securities	Indexed cost column needed Different matching rules	No indexation allowance
Reliefs	Only ROR available Goodwill is not a QBA	Many reliefs are available

Exam focus

You may be required to deal with a chargeable gain computation for either a company or an individual.

It is essential that you are aware of the differences in the way that the gains are calculated.

16

Corporation tax: losses

In this chapter

- Trading losses.
- Carry back relief.
- Carry forward relief.
- Choice of loss relief.
- Pro forma – Trading loss.
- Capital losses.
- Property losses.

Trading losses

- Trading losses for tax purposes are computed in the same way as tax adjusted trading profits.
- Where there is a loss the trading income assessment is £Nil.

The trading loss can be relieved as follows:

- Current year relief.
- Carry back relief.
- Carry forward.

Exam focus

Order of offset

When there is more than one loss to offset:

- deal with the earliest loss first.
- losses brought forward are offset in priority to current year and carry back claims.

Summary of reliefs

Carry forward relief	Current year relief	Carry back relief
		Current year offset first then carry back 12 months
<ul><li>Offset against:<ul><li>First available</li><li>Trading profits</li><li>Of same trade</li></ul></li><li>Indefinite carry forward</li></ul>	<ul><li>Offset against<ul><li>Total profits (income and gains)</li><li>Before QCD relief</li></ul></li><li>Carry forward any remaining losses</li><li>Must offset maximum amount possible if claimed</li><li>QCD relief is lost if no profits to offset against</li><li>Optional claim</li></ul>	

Carry back relief

- Can only be made if there are losses remaining after a current year claim.
- Carry back against total profits before QCD relief of the 12 months preceding the loss making period
  - usually = previous set of accounts
  - if previous accounts < 12 months:
    - (1) carry back 12 months on a LIFO basis, and
    - (2) time apportion profits of earliest accounts.
- Where loss making period is less than 12 months
  - no apportionment is necessary
  - carry back against profits arising in previous 12 months.

- Where a company ceases to trade the loss during the final 12 months of trading:
  - can be carried back, after a current period claim, and
  - offset against the total profits before QCD relief of the preceding 36 months
  - on a LIFO basis.

Exam focus

Exam kit questions in this area:

Constructed response (section C) questions

- Retro Ltd
- Long Ltd and Road Ltd
- Jump Ltd

Carry forward relief

- Future period offsets are:
  - automatic, and
  - against the first available future trading profits
  - from the same trade
  - until all of the available loss has been utilised.
- The only exception to carrying these losses forward indefinitely is if the company changes its trading activity
  - any remaining losses are then forfeited.

Choice of loss relief

Factors influencing choice of loss relief

Cash flow:

- A carry back claim may result in a repayment of tax.
- A carry forward claim will only result in a reduction of future tax.

Qualifying charitable donations:

- Unrelieved QCDs cannot be carried forward.
- Loss relief claims may result in the relief for QCDs being lost.

Pro forma – Trading loss

	2015	2016	2017
	£	£	£
Trading profit	X	0	X
Less: Loss b/f	–		(X)3
	——	——	——
	X	0	X
Other income	X	X	X
Net chargeable gains	X	X	X
Total profits	X	X	X
Less: Loss relief			
– Current year		(X)1	
– Carry back	(X)2		
	——	——	——
	0	0	X
Less: QCD relief	Wasted	Wasted	(X)
	——	——	——
Taxable total profits	0	0	X
	——	——	——

Key Point

2016 is the loss-making year. The trading profit assessment in this year is £Nil.

Keep a separate working for the loss, showing how it is utilised.

Assuming there is sufficient loss available, and assuming that the loss is being relieved as early as possible, the order in which to off-set the loss is as follows:

(1) Current year relief; in the year the loss is made.

(2) Prior year relief; carrying available losses back 12 months.

(3) Carry forward relief; against trading profits only.

Exam focus

Use the loss pro forma to help you adopt a methodical approach to a question involving trading losses.

Approach to loss offset

(1) Lay out years – columnar form.

(2) Calculate TTP ignoring losses.

(3) Choose loss relief by reference to:

- cash flow
  - carry back may result in a repayment of tax
  - carry forward will only result in a reduction of future tax
- offset as soon as possible
- wastage of QCD relief
  - unrelieved amounts cannot be carried forward.

(4) Use separate loss working.

(5) If more than one loss, deal with earliest first.

Capital losses

- Automatically relieved against current year gains.
- Any excess losses are carried forward and relieved against first available future gains.

Capital losses:

- cannot be carried back
- can only be relieved against gains (i.e. not other income).

Property losses

- Property losses are utilised:
  - against total profits, before QCD relief, of the current period
  - any excess losses are relieved against total profits, before QCD relief, of future periods.
- Losses can only be carried forward if the property business is still being carried on.
- The relief is mandatory.
- Property losses are offset before trading losses.

Property losses cannot be carried back.

17

Corporation tax: Groups

In this chapter

- Group relief.
- Capital gains groups.

- When tackling a group question you will need to interpret the group structure from a tax point of view.

  It is important to identify the various groups involved and the reliefs available.

- When revising groups you must learn the definition of a group for each relief and the direction of the relief.

Group relief

- Group loss relief is available to the UK members of a 75% group.
- A group relief group includes the parent company and its 75% subsidiaries.
- Parent company must:
  - have 75% of share capital, and
  - be entitled to 75% of the profits and assets on a winding up.
- Includes indirect holdings, but the parent must have an effective 75% interest in the subsidiary.
- The rules allow group relief groups to be established through companies resident anywhere in the world.
- However, in the F6 examination, loss relief can only be claimed by companies that are resident in the UK.

Reliefs that are available to members of a 75% group relief group

- Any UK company in the group can surrender its loss:
  - to any other UK company in the group
  - in any direction.

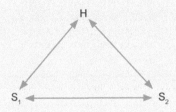

Surrendering company rules

- Losses which may be surrendered are:
  - trading losses
  - unrelieved QCD relief
  - unrelieved property losses.
- Only current year losses can be surrendered.
- QCDs and property losses are 'unrelieved' if they exceed any other income and gains **before** the deduction of any losses.
- The surrendering company can surrender as much of its loss as it likes.
- There is no requirement to relieve the loss against its own profits first.
- Capital losses cannot be group relieved, however a separate relief is available under the capital gains group rules (see later).

Claimant company rules

- The claimant company can only accept losses that it can utilise in the current period:

	£
Total profits (a)	X
Less: Current year losses (b)	(X)
Less: QCD relief	(X)
Maximum loss claim	X

  (a) Total profits for the period after deduction of brought forward losses.
  (b) The company's own losses (if any) are taken into account in computing the maximum group relief claim available. However, relief for the company's own losses need not be actually claimed.

- Group relief is deducted from the claimant company's TTP (i.e. after QCD relief).

Non coterminous accounting periods

- Group relief can be claimed in the corresponding accounting period (CP).

- The CP is the period common to the accounting periods of both the surrendering company and claimant company.

- Profits and losses must be time-apportioned if:
  - the accounting periods are non coterminous, or
  - one company has joined or left the group part way through the period.

- The surrendering company can only surrender the time-apportioned loss of the CP.

- The claimant company can only relieve against time-apportioned TTP for the CP.

- The maximum group relief is therefore the lower of:
  - the loss of the CP, and
  - the TTP of the claimant company of the CP.

Exam focus

Exam kit questions in this area:

OT case (section B) questions:

- Deutsch Ltd

Constructed response (section C) questions:

- Long Ltd and Road Ltd
- Jump Ltd

Due date for group relief claim

- 12 months after the end of the claimant company's filing date for the CAP covered by the claim (i.e. usually 2 years after the end of the CAP).

Payment for group relief

- The claimant company may pay the surrendering company for the loss.
- Any such payment for the group relief is ignored in both companies' CT computations.

Tax loss planning

- Consider:
  - whether to surrender
  - order of surrender.
- Group relief rules are more flexible than rules for using own loss (i.e. can specify amount to be surrendered).

- Restrict amount of group relief to retain sufficient loss to preserve QCD relief or to carry back to generate a repayment of tax.

Key Point

Unlike relief against total profits, group relie is offset against TTP (i.e. after QCD relief). See pro forma computation.

Exam focus

In the past there have been basically two types of group relief written test questions that have been set:

(1) More than one company where we woul need to establish the group structure ar transfer losses in the most tax efficient manner.

(2) Two companies that do not have identic accounting periods.

Capital gains groups

- Group consists of parent company plus 75% subsidiaries.
- Unlike group relief the 75% requirement only applies to the ordinary share capital.
- The subsidiaries can be 75% subsidiaries of 75% subsidiaries but must be effective 51% subsidiaries of the parent company.

  Parent

  | 75% S_2 is 56.25% (0.75×0.75)
  S_1 subsidiary of parent –
  | therefore all are members of
  | 75%   one group

  S_2

- The rules allow groups to be established through companies resident anywhere in the world.

- However, in the F6 examination, the only companies that can take advantage of the capital gains reliefs are:

  - companies resident in the UK.

Implications of gains group

- assets transferred at nil gain/nil loss between group companies
- companies can elect for chargeable gains and allowable capital losses to be transferred from one group company to another
- group ROR.

Assets transferred within the group

- Automatically transferred between companies in the capital gains group at nil gain / nil loss regardless of the price paid.
- Transferee company takes over the asset at cost plus indexation to date of transfer.

Election to transfer chargeable gains or allowable capital losses

- A joint election can be made such that a chargeable gain or allowable capital loss can be transferred from one group company to another
  - provided both were members of the gains group at the time the gain or loss arose.
- Time limit for making the claim = 2 years from the end of the accounting period in which the gain or loss occurs.
- Capital losses cannot be group relieved and cannot be set against other profits of the group, however, the election:
  - allows capital losses and chargeable gains to be matched within a group
  - thus maximising the use of capital losses.

Rollover relief (ROR)

- For ROR purposes all the companies within a capital gains group are treated as carrying on a single trade.

- Therefore a qualifying asset can be sold by one company and the gain can be rolled over into an asset acquired by another company in the group making a qualifying reinvestment within the relevant time period.

Exam focus

Exam kit questions in this area:

Constructed response (section C) questions:

- Heavy Ltd

18

Corporation tax: self-assessment

In this chapter

- Self-assessment.
- Compliance checks.
- Penalties.

Self-assessment

Payment date	
• Normal date • Large company (see below)	• 9 months after end of CAP • 4 quarterly instalments: on 14th of months 7, 10, 13 and 16 after **start** of CAP • Based on estimated liability for the year • Payments must be reviewed and revised as necessary at each instalment date • A company will **not** be required to make quarterly instalments in two circumstances: (1) CT liability is < £10,000 (2) Company not large in previous CAP, and augmented profits ≤ £10 million (÷ number of 51% group companies)
Payment method	• Payment must be made electronically
Filing date	• 12 months after end of period of account • Must be filed electronically along with copies of accounts • Must be filed using Inline eXtensible Business Reporting Language (iXBRL)
Late payment interest Repayment interest	• Charged from due date • Earned from date paid • Charges and receipts are interest expense/income under the loan relationship rules

Retention of records	• 6 years from end of CAP

Large companies

- Large companies must pay corporation tax by instalments (see table above).
- A company is large if its augmented profits for the CAP ≥ £1.5 million (reduced for short APs)

Augmented profits

TTP	X
Dividends received (Note)	X
Augmented profits	X

Note: exclude dividends from 51% group companies

Groups of companies

- The £1.5 million and £10 million thresholds are reduced if a company has any related 51% group companies.
- The number of 51% group companies is determined at the end of the previous CAP.
- Dormant companies are excluded but overseas companies are included.

51% group companies

- Two companies are 51% group companies if:
  - one is a 51% subsidiary of the other, or
  - both are 51% subsidiaries of a third company.
- A 51% subsidiary is one where >50% of share capital is directly or indirectly owned.
- Companies can only be linked by a corporate parent (i.e. not an individual).

Exam focus

It is important that you have a good working knowledge of the self-assessment rules, and in particular, payment dates of tax.

Exam kit questions in this area:

Constructed response (section C) questions

- Clueless Ltd
- E-commerce Ltd
- Lucky Ltd

Compliance Checks

- HMRC must give written notice of their intention to commence a compliance check (enquiry) into a tax return.

- The time limit to make a compliance check is:

  Where a return is submitted on time:

  - 12 months after the actual submission date.

  Where a return is submitted late:

  - 12 months after 31 January, 30 April, 31 July or 31 October following the actual filing date of the return.

- A compliance check ends when HMRC give notice.

- Company has 30 days to amend the return, if applicable.

Amendments and claims for overpayment relief

- A company may amend its return:
  - within 12 months from the filing date.

- HMRC may amend a return:
  - within 9 months from the date the return is filed.

- A company may make a claim for overpayment relief:
  - within four years from the end of the relevant accounting period.

Determination of tax

- Issued by HMRC when a return is not filed by the filing date.
- Can be issued by HMRC within 3 years from filing date (i.e. within 4 years of the end of the period of account).
- Assessment = replaced by the actual self-assessment return when it is submitted.

Discovery assessments, appeals to resolve disputes with HMRC

- Same rules for income tax, corporation tax, capital gains tax, VAT and NIC (Chapter 9).

Penalties

Standard penalties

- same rules for income tax, corporation tax, CGT, VAT and NIC (Chapter 9).

Other penalties for corporation tax

Offence	Penalty
Late filing of corporation tax return: • Within 3 months of filing date • More than 3 months after filing date Additional penalties: • 6-12 months after filing date • More than 12 months after filing date	• Fixed penalty = £100 (Note) • Fixed penalty increased to £200 (Note) • Additional 10% of tax outstanding 6 months after filing date • Additional penalty increased to 20% Note: Fixed penalties rise to £500 and £1,000 if persistently filed late (i.e. return for 2 preceding periods also late).
Failure to keep and retain required records.	Up to £3,000 per accounting period.

19

Value added tax

In this chapter

Exam focus

VAT could be tested in all three sections of the examination.

VAT can be examined in the context of companies or an unincorporated business.

Introduction

- VAT is an indirect tax charged on consumer spending.
- VAT is charged on:
  - a taxable supply
  - by a taxable person
  - in the UK
  - in the course or furtherance of a business.
- Output tax: charged on sales.
- Input tax: incurred on purchases and expenses.

Types of supply

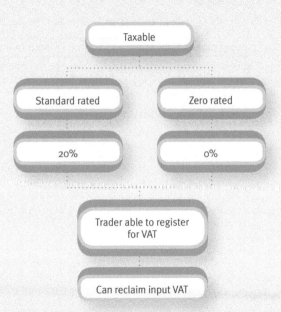

VAT registration

A taxable person is someone who is, or is required to be, registered for VAT.

Compulsory registration	Voluntary registration

• Required when:
  – value of taxable supplies (standard rated or zero rated)
  – exceeds the registration threshold (i.e. £83,000)
	• Traders making taxable supplies (standard rated or zero rated) can register at any time

Compulsory registration

Historic turnover test	Future Test
• Taxable supplies in the last 12 months exceed £83,000	• Taxable supplies in the next 30 days are likely to exceed £83,000
• Perform test at the end of each month	• Perform test constantly
Inform HMRC:	
• Within 30 days of the end of the month in which the threshold is exceeded	• By the end of the 30 day period in which the threshold is expected to be exceeded
Registered from:	
• First day of the second month after the taxable supplies rose above the threshold	• From the start of the 30 day period
• An agreed earlier date	

Exam focus

Exam kit questions in this area:

OT case (section B) questions:

• Candy Apple and Sugar Plum

• Aston Martyn

Constructed response (section C) questions:

• Smart Ltd

Voluntary registration

Advantages	Disadvantages

• Input tax recoverable
• If making zero rated supplies:
   – VAT returns will show VAT repayable
   – can register for monthly returns to aid cash flow
• Avoids penalties for late registration
• May give the impression of a more substantial business
	• Output tax charged on sales:
	   – if make standard rated supplies to customers who are not VAT registered will be an additional cost to them
	   – may affect competitiveness
	• VAT administration burden

Exam focus

Exam kit questions in this area:

OT case (section B) questions:

• The Whitlock sisters

VAT groups

- Membership
  - voluntary.
  - by any UK companies under common control.
- Consequences
  - Representative member responsible for accounting for VAT.
  - No VAT on intra-group sales.
  - Only one VAT return to prepare.
  - All members jointly/severally liable for VAT.

Exam focus

Be prepared to explain whether or not a company should be included in a VAT group.

Deregistration

Compulsory deregistration	Voluntary deregistration
• When cease to make taxable supplies	• If value of expected taxable supplies in the next 12 months will not be > £81,000
Inform HMRC:	
• Within 30 days of ceasing to make taxable supplies	• At any time when above test satisfied
Deregistered from:	
• Date of cessation, or	• Date of request for deregistration, or
• An agreed earlier date	• An agreed later date

- Consequences of deregistration

    - deemed to make a supply of business assets held at date when cease to be a taxable person (e.g. capital items, trading inventory).

    - exclude items if no input tax reclaimed on them (e.g. cars purchased with private use).

    - no output tax charge if VAT on deemed supply is ≤ £1,000.

Tax point

- The tax point is the date that goods/services are supplied.
- Determines:
  - the VAT return period in which the supply is accounted for
  - the rate of VAT (important where there is a change in rate or a change in the classification of a supply).

Basic Tax Point	
Goods: Date goods are available	**Services:** Date services are completed

Basic tax point is changed to	
Earlier Date If payment made, or invoice issued before basic tax point	**Later Date** If invoice is issued within 14 days after basic tax point and an earlier ATP has not already arisen
Actual tax point (ATP): • Date of payment/invoice	Actual tax point: • Date of invoice

Exam focus

Exam kit questions in this area:

OT case (section B) questions:

- The Whitlock Sisters
- Knight Ltd

Constructed response (section C) questions:

- Smart Ltd

VAT returns

- Normally quarterly.
- If receive VAT repayments can elect for monthly returns.
- VAT payable
  = (Total output tax less total input tax).
- All businesses must:
  - file the return online, and
  - pay electronically
  - within one month and seven days of the end of the VAT period.

- VAT inclusive amounts:
  - VAT
    = Gross amount x 20/120 (or 1/6)

  - Net amount
    = Gross amount x 100/120.

Output VAT

Value of supply

- Consideration in money
    - trader's VAT exclusive selling price less the amount of any discounts applied.
- Consideration not in money, or money and something other than money:
    - Open market value.
- Gifts of inventory and non-current assets:
    - Replacement value.
- Certain gifts are not taxable supplies:
    - goods which cost ≤ £50 per customer, per year, and
    - any number of business samples and gifts of services (to employees or customers).
- Goods for own use:
    - Replacement value if purchased for business purposes (no output VAT if purchased for private purposes).

Relief for impairment losses

- Relief available where:
    - Output VAT in respect of an outstanding debt has been accounted for and paid by the supplier.
    - The supplier has written the debt off in the accounts as irrecoverable.
    - Six months has elapsed since the debt was due for payment.
- Claim the relief as input VAT on the VAT return.

Exam focus

Exam kit questions in this area:

OT case (section B) questions:

- Knight Ltd

Constructed response (section C) questions:

- Garfield
- Glacier Ltd
- Zim

Transfer of a going concern (TOGC)

- Transfer of a business is not treated as a taxable supply for VAT purposes, therefore:
  - no output VAT charged on assets transferred by seller
  - no input VAT recoverable by purchaser.
- Conditions:
  - business transferred as a going concern
  - no significant break in trading
  - to a taxable person (VAT registered or liable to become VAT registered)
  - same type of trade carried on after the transfer.
- The transferee may:
  - take over VAT registration of the transferor, but
  - also inherits the transferor's VAT liabilities.

- Where there is a transfer of a business which is not a going concern, or where the transferee is not a taxable person:
  - VAT is payable on the individual assets transferred.

Input VAT

- Conditions to reclaim input VAT:
  - Must be taxable person when incurred
    (exception = pre-registration VAT).
  - Supply must have been to the person making the claim.
  - Supply must be properly supported, normally by VAT invoice.
  - Goods/services must be used for business purposes.
- No distinction between capital and revenue expenditure
  - input VAT is recoverable on the purchase of capital assets as well as revenue expenditure.

Non-deductible VAT

- Business entertainment
  - Includes hospitality of any kind (e.g. food, drink, accommodation).
  - Excludes entertaining overseas customers and staff entertainment.
- Motor cars
  - Purchase – only recoverable if used 100% for business.
  - Leasing – if partly used for private purposes, only 50% of VAT on leasing charge recoverable.
  - Motor expenses – provided some business use, 100% recoverable.
  - If input VAT is not recovered on purchase, no output VAT is charged on disposal.

- Fuel – Input tax 100% deductible even if private fuel provided. Output VAT chargeable on:
  - fuel reimbursed in full
    - amount reimbursed
  - not reimbursed at all
    - fuel scale charge
  - partially reimbursed
    - not examinable.
- Private use
  - input VAT cannot be claimed on goods or services not used for business purposes
  - an apportionment is made for partial private use.
- Goods for own use:
  - input VAT recoverable if purchased for business purposes (and output VAT is due as above)
  - input VAT not recoverable if purchased for private purposes (and no output VAT is due).

Key Point

Where VAT is not recoverable on capital expenditure (e.g. purchase of a car), capital allowances are claimed on the VAT inclusive cost.

Exam focus

Exam kit questions in this area:

OT case (section B) questions:

- Knight Ltd

Constructed response (section C) questions

- Garfield
- Glacier Ltd
- Zim

Pre-registration input VAT

Conditions to reclaim input VAT:

Goods	Services
• Acquired in the 4 years before registration, and • Still held at date of registration	• Supplied in the 6 months before registration

Special accounting schemes

- Three special schemes aimed at small businesses.

Cash accounting scheme

Operation	Conditions	Advantages
• VAT accounted for on cash payments and cash receipts	• Taxable turnover ≤ £1,350,000 • VAT payments and returns must be up to date • Must leave the scheme if taxable turnover > £1,600,000	• Do not pay output tax until receive payment from customer • Provides automatic relief for irrecoverable debts

Exam focus

Exam kit questions in this area:

Constructed response (section C) questions:

- Silverstone Ltd
- Smart Ltd
- Garfield

Flat rate scheme

Operation	Conditions	Advantages
• Flat rate of VAT applied to total VAT inclusive turnover (including exempt supplies & VAT) • Flat rate determined by trade sector • Flat rate only used to simplify preparation of VAT return – still need to issue tax invoices	• Taxable supplies for the next 12 months ≤ £150,000 • Businesses are eligible to stay in the scheme until their annual income exceeds £230,000	• Reduces administration – do not need to account for VAT on individual purchases • May reduce total VAT payable

Exam focus

Exam kit questions in this area:

OT case (section B) questions:

• The Whitlock Sisters

Constructed response (section C) questions:

• Zim

Annual accounting scheme

Operation	Conditions	Advantages

• One VAT return prepared a year
• Return due:
  2 months after end of annual VAT period
• Payments on account (POA):
  – 9 POA due in months 4 – 12
  – each POA is 10% of VAT for previous year
• Balancing payment due with the VAT return
• New businesses base POA on estimated VAT liability
	• Taxable turnover ≤ £1,350,000
	• VAT payments and returns must be up to date
	• Must leave the scheme if taxable turnover > £1,600,000
		• Reduces administration
		• Regular payments can help budgeting and cash flow

Exam focus

Exam kit questions in this area:

Constructed response (section C) questions:

- Silverstone Ltd
- Garfield

VAT administration

VAT invoices

- Must issue a VAT invoice within 30 days of the date of the supply.
- Can be sent electronically if customer agrees.
- Exceptions:
  - Supplies are zero rated.
  - Customer is not VAT registered.
- Evidence for reclaiming input VAT.
- Must contain:
  - identifying number
  - date of issue
  - tax point
  - supplier's name, address and VAT registration number
  - customer's name and address
  - description of goods/services

- for each description:
  - quantity
  - price/item (excluding VAT)
  - rate of VAT
  - rate of discount offered
- total amount payable (excluding VAT)
- total VAT payable.
- Less detailed VAT invoices can be provided for supplies valued up to £250.

Exam focus

Exam kit questions in this area:

OT case (section B) questions:

- Candy Apple and Sugar Plum

Constructed response (section C) questions:

- Glacier Ltd

VAT records

Must keep records of all goods/services received and supplied, sufficient to allow the return to be completed and allow HMRC to check the return.

- Retain records for 6 years.
- Type of records to retain:
  - copies of VAT invoices issued
  - record of outputs (e.g. sales day book)
  - evidence to support recovery of input tax
  - VAT account.

Discovery assessments and appeals to resolve disputes with HMRC

- Same rules for income tax, corporation tax, capital gains tax, VAT and NIC (Chapter 9).

VAT penalties

- Standard penalty applies in the same way for income tax, CGT, corporation tax and VAT.
- Depends on the behaviour of the taxpayer (Chapter 9).
- Errors in VAT returns can give rise to
  - Default interest, and
  - Standard penalty for the submission of an incorrect VAT return.
- Specific penalty relating to VAT is:
  - the default surcharge.

Exam focus

Exam kit questions in this area:

OT case (section B) questions:

- Knight Ltd

Constructed response (section C) questions:

- Tardy plc
- Glacier Ltd

Default surcharge

Arises	<ul><li>Return submitted late, or</li><li>VAT paid late</li></ul>	
First default	<ul><li>HMRC serve a surcharge liability notice</li><li>Specifies a surcharge period: – ending 12 months after the end of the VAT period to which the default relates</li></ul>	
Further defaults	<ul><li>Surcharge period extended to 12 months after the end of the VAT period to which the latest default relates</li><li>If default involves late payment of VAT – Surcharge penalty levied</li></ul>	
Surcharges	**Default in surcharge period**	**% of VAT unpaid**
	First	2%
	Second	5%
	Third	10%
	Fourth and more	15%

Note:

- Surcharge assessments at rates below 10% will not be issued for amounts of ≤ £400.
- Where rate is 10% or more, the minimum surcharge is £30.

Error on VAT returns

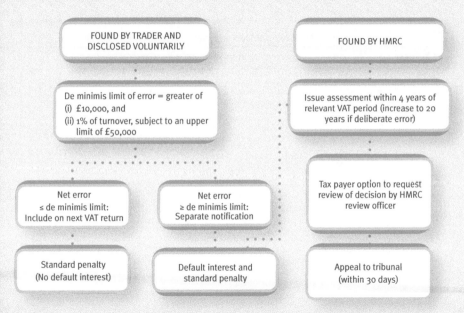

FOUND BY TRADER AND DISCLOSED VOLUNTARILY

FOUND BY HMRC

De minimis limit of error = greater of
(i) £10,000, and
(ii) 1% of turnover, subject to an upper limit of £50,000

Issue assessment within 4 years of relevant VAT period (increase to 20 years if deliberate error)

Net error ≤ de minimis limit: Include on next VAT return

Net error ≥ de minimis limit: Separate notification

Tax payer option to request review of decision by HMRC review officer

Standard penalty (No default interest)

Default interest and standard penalty

Appeal to tribunal (within 30 days)

Default interest

Arises	• HMRC raise an assessment to collect undeclared/over claimed VAT
	• Voluntary disclosure of errors exceeding de minimis limit
Charged	• From due date of payment to actual date of payment

Overseas aspects of VAT

Different VAT treatment depending on whether or not transaction is in EU.

EU transactions for goods

Status of parties	Supplier and customer VAT registered (i.e. business to business) (B2B)
Rate of VAT	Country of origin • zero rated Destination country • rate applicable in destination country (reverse charge procedure)
Supplier	No VAT (as supply zero rated)
Customer	Pays output VAT based on date of acquisition, which is the ealier of: • date of invoice and • 15th day of month following month goods came into UK Claims VAT suffered as input VAT

Non-EU transactions for supply of goods

Imports

- Importer pays VAT at point of entry into UK.
- Can pay monthly through Duty Deferment System.
- Recovers VAT suffered as input tax.
- Net effect is the same as for purchases from the UK.

Exports

- All goods are zero rated.

Key Point

All supplies of goods whether within or outside the EU = taxable supplies.

Issue = whether the supply is standard or zero rated.

It will never be an exempt supply.

Net effect on purchases from within or outside the EU same, unless purchaser makes exempt supplies.

Exam focus

Exam kit questions in this area:

Constructed response (section C) questions:

- Silverstone Ltd
- Garfield

Supply of services

Where services are supplied to a business customer VAT is charged where the customer is established.

These rules can be applied to B2B transactions involving a UK business as follows:

UK business		Accounting for VAT
Supplies services to	• Overseas business customer	• Place of supply is overseas. • Outside the scope of UK VAT.

Receives services from	• Overseas business	• Place of supply is UK.
		• Reverse charge procedure:
		  – UK business accounts for 'output VAT' at standard UK rate on VAT return.
		  – This VAT can then be reclaimed as input VAT.

Exam focus

Exam kit questions in this area:

Constructed response (section C) questions:

- Tardy plc

20

Scenario style
section C questions

In this chapter

- Scenario question style.
- Comparison of two alternative options.
- Calculation of tax in the margin.
- Multi-tax questions.

Scenario question style

- Scenario style questions are intended to make students think about tax consequences of actions and start to develop higher tax planning skills.

- This style of exam question can include one or more of the following elements:

  - more individual parts to the question with smaller mark allocations

  - more written requirements, rather than just calculations

  - information provided in a less obvious way

  - comparison of two alternative options, with different tax implications

  - calculations of tax at a taxpayer's effective marginal rate of tax

  - combination of more than one type of tax in the same question

  - consideration of tax advantages of certain transactions.

- Note that the actual calculations required tend to be fairly straightforward, however analytic skills are required.

Exam focus

Exam kit questions in this area:

Constructed response (section C) questions

- Sophia Wong
- Ginger and Nigel
- Mick Stone
- Ruby
- Pere Jones
- Richard Tryer
- Kendra Older

Comparison of two alternative options

- Question 4 in December 2010 compared taking a company car versus additional remuneration.

- Question 1(b) in June 2011 compared the choice of taking on a partner or a new employee.

- Question 4(a) in December 2012 compared the total tax suffered by taking all the profits from a new company as director's remuneration or as dividends with the total tax suffered as a self-employed individual.

- Question 3(b) in June 2013 required the comparison of disposing of two different warehouses. Part (c) required the comparison of a husband or wife disposing of shares.

- Question 3 in June 2014 required calculating CGT with and without the application of reliefs.

- These questions also involved the consideration of different taxes in relation to the same scenario, such as IT, NICs and CT.

- A comparative scenario may ask you to look at the after tax net costs, rather than just the tax cost of the alternatives.

Calculation of tax in the margin

- Question 2(d) in June 2010 required students to calculate the additional IT and NIC due on additional remuneration paid to a director.

- Question 4 in December 2010 required students to calculate the IT and NICs due on both a company car and additional director's remuneration.

- Question 1(c) in December 2011 required students to calculate the income tax reductions for two taxpayers, if further personal pension contributions were paid by one and company car contributions allocated more favourably for the other.

- Although these questions could be answered by preparing full tax computations

  - you are expected to calculate the answers using the individuals' marginal rates of tax

  - the marks (and therefore time available) were allocated accordingly.

- 'Working in the margin' is an important skill in taxation you need to be able to

  - identify whether an individual is a basic, higher or additional rate taxpayer, and

  - calculate the tax on additional income at the appropriate rate.

  This is the only way to achieve the marks in the time available.

Multi-tax questions

- In the past more than one tax has been examined but usually as independent parts of a question.

- Some of the comparison of two alternative option questions however involve IT, NICs and CT.

- Question 5 in June 2013 was unusual as it required the IHT, IT and CGT liabilities of a father and son from just one set of information.

- Question 5(b) in June 2014 required consideration of both CGT and IHT in relation to the same gift.

Tips for success

- Stop and think before writing your answer.

- Make sure you are clear as to what the examining team is asking you to do and that you have identified the simplest way to calculate it.

- Make sure you have spotted all the information the examining team has given you. For example, in Q4 December 2012, the examining team provided the figure for director's remuneration after allowing for employer's class 1 NIC, and since all the profits were withdrawn, the class 1 NIC figure was the difference between the profits and the director's remuneration. Equally, the figure for dividends after allowing for corporation tax was given and therefore the corporation tax liability was the balancing figure. Both these figures could be calculated from the information given, but this would waste valuable time.

- Where there are a number of small parts to a question:
  - make sure you plan your time well, and
  - attempt all parts of the question.

- Lots of requirements can help to provide advice on your approach to the answer:
  - they should be seen as guidance on what to cover, and
  - the requirements are usually very clear, and not misleading.

- Play close attention to any guidance provided by the examining team regarding how to approach the question and which calculations to include.

- Use common sense
  - look at the mark allocation and think about your approach accordingly.

- A two mark question:
    - usually requires 2 or 4 key points/ steps,
    - should only take 3-4 minutes
    - should not generate a page of answers!
- Do not waste time doing unnecessary calculations.
- Short workings can appear on the face of the computation and do not need to be on a separate page.
- Make sure answers are easy to follow and easy to mark – do not cram answers on one page.
- Use headings for each separate part of your answer, especially different taxes, and do not try to combine your calculations into one.
- Draw conclusions where you are asked to – not doing so can miss a mark even if your calculations are correct.

Index

V

W

Z